T0319897

Trade Liberalisation
and
The Poverty of Nations

Other Books by A.P. Thirlwall

Growth and Development: with Special Reference to Developing Economies (1972; Eighth Edition, 2006)

Inflation, Saving and Growth in Developing Countries (1974)

Regional Growth and Unemployment in the UK (*with R. Dixon*, 1975)

Financing Economic Development (1976)

Keynes and International Monetary Relations (edited, 1976)

Keynes and Laissez Faire (edited, 1978)

Keynes and the Bloomsbury Group (edited *with D. Crabtree*, 1980)

Balance of Payments Theory and the UK Experience (1980; Fourth Edition *with H. Gibson*, 1992)

Keynes as a Policy Adviser (edited, 1982)

Keynes and Economic Development (edited, 1987)

Nicholas Kaldor (1987)

Deindustrialisation (1989 *with S. Bazen*: Third Edition, 1997)

Further Essays on Economic Theory and Policy, Volume 9 by Nicholas Kaldor (edited *with F. Targetti*, 1989)

The Essential Kaldor (edited *with F. Targetti*, 1989)

European Factor Mobility: Trends and Consequences (edited *with I. Gordon*, 1989)

The Performance and Prospects of the Pacific Island Economies in the World Economy (1991)

Keynes and the Role of the State (edited *with D. Crabtree*, 1993)

Economic Growth and the Balance of Payments Constraint (*with J. McCombie*, 1994)

The Economics of Growth and Development: Selected Essays of A.P. Thirlwall, Volume 1 (1995)

Causes of Growth and Stagnation in the World Economy (the Mattioli Lectures by N. Kaldor) (edited *with F. Targetti*, 1995)

Macroeeconomic Issues from a Keynesian Perspective: Selected Essays of A.P. Thirlwall, Volume 2 (1997)

Economic Dynamics, Trade and Growth: Essays on Harrodian Themes (edited *with G. Rampa and L. Stella*, 1998)

The Euro and Regional Divergence in Europe (2000)

The Nature of Economic Growth: An Alternative Framework for Understanding the Performance of Nations (2002)

Trade, the Balance of Payments and Exchange Rate Policy in Developing Countries (2003)

Essays on Balance of Payments Constrained Growth: Theory and Evidence (*with J. McCombie*, 2004)

Trade Liberalisation
and
The Poverty of Nations

A.P. Thirlwall

Professor of Applied Economics, University of Kent, Canterbury, UK

and

Penélope Pacheco-López

Economic Consultant

Edward Elgar
Cheltenham, UK • Northampton, MA, USA

Published by
Edward Elgar Publishing Limited
The Lypiatts
15 Lansdown Road
Cheltenham
Glos GL50 2JA
UK

Edward Elgar Publishing, Inc.
William Pratt House
9 Dewey Court
Northampton
Massachusetts 01060
USA

A catalogue record for this book
is available from the British Library

Library of Congress Control Number: 2008932908

ISBN 978 1 84720 822 4 (cased)

Printed and bound in Great Britain by MPG Books Ltd, Bodmin, Cornwall

Contents

Acknowledgements

The authors are very grateful to Dr Ha-Joon Chang, Professor Robert Wade and Professor Dani Rodrik for allowing them to use sections of books and articles written by them in abridged form:

Ha-Joon Chang (2002), *Kicking Away the Ladder: Development Strategy in Historical Perspective* (London: Anthem Press).
R. Wade (2004), Is Globalisation Reducing Poverty and Inequality?, *World Development*, April.
D. Rodrik (2001), *The Global Governance of Trade: As if Development Really Mattered* (New York: UNDP).

We would also like to thank all the 'team' at Edward Elgar – Matthew Pitman, Elizabeth Clack and Nep Elverd – for all their help in seeing the book through the press.

Preface

The purpose of this book is to argue that trade liberalisation, with the ultimate objective of free trade, is not in the interest of poor developing countries at their present stage of economic and social development. History, economic theory and contemporary statistical evidence does not support the view that trade liberalisation, or making economies more open, necessarily raises the growth of living standards, reduces poverty or leads to a more equal, fairer, distribution of income between countries in the world or between people within countries. The orthodox theory of trade liberalisation is therefore being sold by international institutions to developing countries on a false prospectus.

The book is the last of a trilogy of short, readable books which attempt to provide an alternative approach to that of orthodox neoclassical trade and growth theory for an understanding of the growth and development process, with particular reference to poor developing countries. The first book, *The Nature of Economic Growth: An Alternative Framework for Understanding the Performance of Nations* (Thirlwall, 2002) presents a structural, demand-constrained model of growth, in contrast to the one-sector supply-oriented growth model of orthodox neoclassical theory, in which the balance of payments or foreign exchange is identified as the major constraint on growth, and the structure of production is crucial because different goods have different production and demand characteristics. The second book, *Trade, the Balance of Payments and Exchange Rate Policy in Developing Countries* (Thirlwall, 2003) focuses on the neglect of the balance of payments (or monetary) consequences of trade in orthodox trade and growth theory and casts doubt on whether exchange rate devaluation, or depreciation of the currency, is an efficient balance of payments adjustment weapon.

This new book continues to question the orthodoxy proposed by mainstream academic economists, and policymakers in international institutions such as the International Monetary Fund (IMF), World Bank and World Trade Organization (WTO), that trade liberalisation is the panacea, or magic bullet, that will launch poor developing countries on to a higher growth path consistent with balance of payments equilibrium. We argue that what we witness in the world economy today, in an era of unprecedented trade liberalisation, resembles much more closely the predictions of non-orthodox models of growth and development that highlight cumulative processes and polarisation between people and countries, rather than the equalising, equilibrating predictions of orthodox neoclassical trade and growth theory.

The prevailing consensus in the years since the Second World War has been that if countries are to develop and prosper they must liberalise their trade, almost at any cost. Free trade has become a mantra. The orthodoxy has a long and distinguished ancestory that goes back at least to Adam Smith's famous book, *An Inquiry into the Nature and Causes of the Wealth of Nations* (1776) and David Ricardo's *On The Principles of Political Economy and Taxation* (1817), but it was given renewed impetus after the Second World War following the great depression and the beggar-thy-neighbour policies (protectionism) experienced during the 1930s. At the Bretton Woods Conference convened in 1944, which established the IMF and the World Bank, the world's major economies committed themselves to a liberal, free trade, order, endorsed in the 1980s by the so-called Washington Consensus, and reinforced by the establishment of the WTO in 1995.

There is no doubt that there are real resource gains from trade, as Smith and Ricardo originally showed, but there is nothing in the doctrine of free trade, or in the practice of liberalising trade, to guarantee an equal distribution of the gains from trade among participating countries or between individuals within countries. Indeed, in certain circumstances, which are not so unusual, such as terms of trade deterioration and balance of payments problems, countries may suffer absolute real income losses from specialisation according to the law of comparative advantage. Nor is there anything in the doctrine of free trade that guarantees a *permanent* increase in the rate of growth of output and living standards. On the contrary, it is an interesting and pertinent fact that despite extensive trade liberalisation, the economies of many countries, particularly those in Africa and Latin America, have performed very poorly in the last 20 years or so, and world income inequality has worsened – ignoring the fast growth of China. The Gini ratio, as a measure of income distribution across countries of the world (international inequality) and across peoples of the world (global inequality), is as high today (if not higher) as it was in the 1960s. Only a handful of poor developing countries (mainly in Asia) have narrowed the relative income gap between themselves and the rich developed countries. The vast majority of developing countries continue to lag behind, and many African countries are absolutely poorer today than they were 30 years ago. Does this mean that these countries do not trade enough, that their trade needs to be more liberal, or is there something wrong with the doctrine of free trade? It is also interesting and significant that while international organisations and rich developed countries preach free trade to developing countries, the rich countries themselves do not practice what they preach, and never did so historically when they were attempting to industrialise and develop (Chang, 2002). The basic problem with the free trade orthodoxy is that it brushes to one side the different production and demand characteristics of different types of goods, and assumes continuous full employment so that in the reorganisation of resources that specialisation and trade bring about there is no permanent unemployment; everyone finds a job. In practice, however, some goods (for example, land-based activities) are produced under conditions of diminishing returns, while others are produced under conditions of increasing returns. This makes a profound difference to the growth of living standards in countries specialising in these different types of activity. Also, some goods (for example, primary commodities) have a low income elasticity of demand in world trade, while others have a high income elasticity of demand. This makes a significant difference to the rate at which exports and imports grow in different countries specialising in different types of activity. There is a crucial link between the structure of production and trade and the economic performance that can be expected from trade liberalisation, which the orthodoxy ignores. In many circumstances, trade liberalisation may not be optimal for developing countries, at least without the implementation of complementary measures such as export promotion policies, strategic investment in structural change, infant industry protection and supportive exchange rate policies. The speed and sequencing of liberalisation measures are also important to bear in mind.

In the book we attempt to bring together in a readable and coherent way the vast literature that now exists on the theory, practice and impact of trade liberalisation – for the benefit of students, policymakers, and all those interested in what is happening to developing economies as the world economy becomes more liberalised and globalised (to use the fashionable terminology). The book has three essential messages:

1. Trade liberalisation is neither a necessary nor sufficient condition for the more rapid development of poor countries, when development is defined in its broad sense (Goulet, 1971, 1995) of not only providing life sustenance for its people, but also self-esteem and freedom. If trade liberalisation does not reduce poverty, that is not development. If trade liberalisation leaves countries more dependent on others because trade is 'unequal', that is not development. If pressure to liberalise trade reduces countries' freedom to pursue their own economic policies, that is not development.

2. Neo-liberal economics, which puts faith in trade liberalisation as the route to development, has become like a religion or creed, which not only ignores perfectly respectable economic theory which shows that there are several legitimate economic arguments for protection, but also disregards history and the facts of experience of how today's developed countries progressed in the 19th century and the first half of the 20th century, and the miserable contemporary experience of many of today's developing countries that have been forced by multilateral institutions to liberalise prematurely or too quickly.

3. The extensive empirical research on the impact of trade liberalisation on exports, imports,

the balance of payments and growth does not support the view that liberalisation, at least since the 1980s, has been associated with a superior economic performance of poor countries, or a narrowing of the degree of international income inequality between countries and peoples of the world. The view to the contrary, espoused by neo-liberal economists and international institutions, is largely dependent on the inclusion of China and India in the sample of poor countries taken by investigators. These are two poor populous countries, which have grown very fast in the last 20 years, and where trade as a proportion of GDP has grown very rapidly, and they naturally make a huge difference to the statistical results relating to trade and growth and trade and income inequality. But China and India are just two of over 150 poor, developing countries. If they are excluded from the sample of poor, 'globalising' economies, a different picture of the world is painted – one in which international and global inequality is rising, where the number of people living on less than $2 a day is rising, and 'globalising' countries are performing no better on average than those which are not liberalising their economies so fast. Individual case studies show a variety of experience.

We argue, therefore, that the rhetoric of trade liberalisation, as a necessary condition for development and poverty reduction, is not matched by the reality.

The choice is not between autarchy and free trade, but the sensible management of trade: to achieve a balance between the growth of exports and imports so as to avoid balance of payments deficits; to allow policy space for poor countries to identify and encourage new areas of comparative advantage; to enable the State to intervene to promote 'self-discovery' (Hausmann and Rodrik, 2003); and to allow a judicious mix of tariffs and subsidies for infant industry protection. This is the way rich countries developed historically, and it is the way that poor developing countries today should be allowed to develop. In an environment of *laissez-faire, laissez-passer*, structural change is impossible.

In Chapter 1 we briefly rehearse the theory of trade liberalisation, and the benefits that it is supposed to confer on countries, and then outline the various meanings and measures of trade liberalisation that investigators have used in their research. Then we challenge the orthodoxy in a formal way, and consider history.

Chapter 2 focuses on the trade performance of countries that have liberalised, but not just the effect of liberalisation on exports which is the conventional approach. The effect of liberalisation on imports and the balance of payments is also considered, which can act as a constraint on economic performance. We survey the vast amount of research that has been conducted on trade liberalisation and economic growth, both within countries using time-series data, and across countries using cross-section and panel data.

In Chapter 3 we discuss unorthodox models that predict growing inequality with trade and we give evidence of the degree of income inequality in the world economy between rich and poor countries, using measures of international inequality (which take the average per capita income of each country) and global inequality (which takes account of the distribution of income within countries as well).

Chapter 4 examines research on the link between trade liberalisation in developing countries and poverty, wage inequality, and the personal distribution of income using household survey data. Orthodoxy predicts a narrowing of the domestic income distribution within poor countries, but the reality is different.

Chapter 5 draws some policy conclusions on how trade policy should proceed in the interests of the poorer, developing nations of the world, and of poor people within poor countries. There are national issues to consider, and also international issues relating to how international economic relations are organised and conducted relating to trade in goods and services, capital flows and financial arrangements between rich and poor countries, in the interests of a fairer distribution of income in the world economy between countries and people.

1. The theory and measurement of trade liberalisation

> Politicians and economists who promise that trade liberalisation will make everyone better off are being disingenuous. Economic theory (and historical experience) suggests the contrary. (Stiglitz, 2006)

Introduction

To consider the relationship between trade liberalisation and economic development, it is important to state at the outset what we mean by the process of economic development. The traditional measure of economic development, and what the theory of trade liberalisation focuses on, is the standard of living measured by the average level of per capita income of the citizens of a country. The static gains from trade liberalisation are supposed to raise the *level* of income in the process of resource reallocation according to the law of comparative advantage; and the dynamic gains from trade, associated with more competition, the flow of new knowledge and a faster rate of capital accumulation, are supposed to raise the *growth* of income. The focus on national income, or on the growth of income, as a measure of development is not enough, however, for two main reasons. Firstly, what happens to the distribution of income within countries matters for the measurement of economic welfare. Trade liberalisation does not guarantee that all sectors of society will benefit equally. On the contrary, in the very process of liberalisation itself some groups will gain, but others, previously protected, will undoubtedly lose either relatively or absolutely through unemployment or a reduction in their real income. While total income and average per capita income may rise, a distribution-weighted measure of per capita income which gives a higher weight to the losses of already poor people than to the gains of already rich people may show a loss of welfare. Secondly, what happens to the international distribution of income is also important. Trade liberalisation does not guarantee an equal distribution of the gains from trade between countries. Some countries will benefit more than others, depending on their competitive strength in world markets, and movements in the terms of trade. If rich countries gain more than poor countries, the international distribution of income will worsen. The gains of some rich countries may even be at the expense of other (poorer) countries that lose absolutely. As the German Chancellor, Otto Von Bismark, once remarked 'free trade is a policy for the strong'!

The eminent French sociologist, Denis Goulet, defines economic and social development in terms of three core components, which he calls life sustenance, self-esteem and freedom (Goulet, 1971,

1995). Life sustenance refers to the provision of basic human needs such as food, shelter and clothing. A country that cannot provide basic needs for all its people cannot be considered as developed. A country in which poverty is increasing is not developing. As Stiglitz argues in his powerful book, *Making Globalization Work* (2006), 'if economic growth is not shared throughout society, then development has failed – development is about transforming the lives of people, not just transforming countries'. Trade liberalisation that creates poverty is anti-developmental. Self-esteem refers to feelings of independence and self-worth. A country is not fully developed if it lacks self-esteem because it is unable to conduct economic relations on equal terms. Trade liberalisation that makes a poor country more dependent on richer countries for international aid, or on international institutions, such as the IMF, for loans, is not developed. Likewise, an economy that comes to be dominated by multinational corporations in key sectors of the economy, which destroy local industries, or which has its banking sector taken over by foreign banks, cannot be said to be developing. Freedom is about countries and people being able to decide their own destiny. No country or persons are free if they cannot chose, because they are dependent on others for aid and assistance and economic policymaking is outside their democratic control (see also Sen, 1999). Trade liberalisation that locks countries into unfavourable economic structures based on static comparative advantage, which perpetuates slow growth and poverty, is not a development strategy.

The key issue from a development perspective, therefore, is not whether trade liberalisation improves the growth performance of a country, although that is important, but whether it reduces poverty; whether it raises the income of poor people relative to the rich, and whether it enhances the ability of poor countries to catch up with the rich. These are the issues to constantly bear in mind in discussing the practice and merits of trade liberalisation. But first let us discuss the theory and measurement of liberalisation, and some of the theoretical challenges to the orthodoxy.

The 'Classical' Foundations of Trade Liberalisation

The doctrine that trade enhances welfare and growth has a long and distinguished ancestry dating back at least to the great classical economists of Adam Smith (1723–90), David Ricardo (1772–1823) and John Stuart Mill (1806–73). In his famous book, *An Inquiry into the Nature and Causes of the Wealth of Nations* (1776), Smith stressed the role of trade as a vent, or outlet, for surplus domestic production, and as a means of widening the market, thereby allowing greater specialisation or division of labour. Specialisation, in turn, stimulates capital accumulation and promotes 'learning by doing'. Remember Smith's famous dictum that 'specialisation is limited by the extent of the market', but that is only one side of the coin. The extent of the market is determined, in turn, by the division of labour because it is the latter that raises productivity and purchasing power. As well as static economies of scale from specialisation, therefore, there is also the prospect that more trade will enhance *growth* by inducing so-called 'dynamic economies of scale' associated with capital accumulation, technical progress embodied in capital, and the spread of knowledge. To quote Smith directly:

> Between places foreign trade is carried on, they all of them derive two distinct benefits from it. It carries out that surplus part of the produce of their land and labour for which there is no demand among them, and brings back in return for it something else for which there is a demand. It gives a value to their superfluities, by exchanging them for something else, which may satisfy a part of their wants and increase their enjoyments. By means of it, the narrowness of the home market does not hinder the division of labour in any particular branch of art or manufacture from being carried to the highest perfection. By opening a more extensive market for whatever part of the produce of their labour may exceed the home consumption, it encourages them to improve its productive powers and to augment its annual produce to the utmost, and thereby to increase the real revenue and wealth of the society. (p. 338)

In 1817, Ricardo published his *On The Principles of Political Economy and Taxation* in which the basis of trade is not vent for surplus commodities expanding the market and permitting specialisation, as in Smith, but differences in the productivity of labour (or relative costs) between countries in the production of different goods. This leads to the idea of comparative advantage. A country may have an *absolute* productivity (cost) advantage in the production of *every* good, but according to Ricardo's remarkable theorem[1] it will still pay a country to specialise in those commodities in which it has a *comparative* advantage, that is in those commodities in which relative labour productivity is the highest or for which the *opportunity cost* of production is lowest. Ricardo is not explicit about what determines relative differences in productivity and costs, but clearly resource endowments will be the major determinants: natural resources, labour, human capital and the level of technology. To illustrate the gains from trade, according to the law of comparative advantage, Ricardo used the example of England specialising in cloth and Portugal in wine, so we shall do the same. England has a natural advantage in the production of cloth, and Portugal has a natural advantage in the production of wine. Suppose that in England the opportunity cost ratio between cloth and wine is 10:1 (with cloth measured in yards and wine in bottles), whereas in Portugal it is only 4:1. This means that if England wanted to produce 1000 bottles of wine it would have to sacrifice 10 000 yards of cloth, whereas if Portugal produced 1000 bottles of wine it would sacrifice only 4000 yards of cloth. On the other hand, if England produced 1000 yards of cloth, it would sacrifice only 100 bottles of wine, whereas if Portugal wanted to produce 1000 yards of cloth it would sacrifice 250 bottles of wine.

Clearly, the opportunity cost of producing wine in England is greater than in Portugal, and the opportunity cost of producing cloth in Portugal is higher than in England. If there was an international rate of exchange between England and Portugal between the two internal rates of exchange of 10:1 and 4:1, both countries could benefit from specialising in what they are best at producing in an opportunity cost sense, and exchanging goods at a more favourable rate of transformation internationally than domestically. For example, if the international rate of exchange of cloth for wine was, say, 7:1, England could now get more wine per unit of cloth 'sacrificed' and Portugal could get more cloth per unit of wine. Both countries would benefit from specialising and trading the surplus of production over domestic consumption. To use technical language, by trading, the consumption possibility frontier would lie outside the domestic production possibility frontier for both countries. Ricardo's theorem is a very powerful one, and has been extremely influential because it lies at the heart of the free trade doctrine that countries will always benefit if they liberalise trade. Those who invoke Ricardo, and the law of comparative advantage, in support of trade liberalisation, however, often forget (intentionally or otherwise) to mention its implicit assumptions and flaws which considerably weaken its appeal. Two main points will be emphasised here: first its static nature and its indifference to the types of goods that countries specialise in, and secondly, the assumptions of continuous full employment and balanced trade.

The law of comparative advantage is 'static' because the resource (consumption) gains from a country moving from self-sufficiency to specialisation and then trade are 'once-for-all'. They do not recur. Once a country has liberalised, and the process of resource allocation between activities has taken place, there are no further gains. In other words, the comparative cost doctrine by itself has no predictions about economic growth. The gains from trade are not dynamic; they do not necessarily launch a country on a higher *growth* path. The growth of economies through time depends on *what* countries specialise in producing, not on the process of specialisation itself, because some activities have higher potential growth rates than others. The theory of comparative advantage has nothing to say about productivity growth and its sources. It may benefit Portugal to specialise in wine in a static sense, but labour productivity growth in viniculture may be inherently lower than in cloth because there is not so much scope for economies of scale or technical progress. Indeed, viniculture is almost certainly a diminishing returns activity because land suitable for wine production is in fixed supply. In this case, Portugal is condemned to a slower growth of its economy than England which specialises in cloth, which is an increasing returns activity because all factors of production are variable.

What has been said in this example of Portugal is true for many developing countries today that still specialise in the production of primary commodities which are land-based activities subject to diminishing returns. More than 50 per cent of the export earnings of developing countries come from primary commodities (and 70 per cent in Africa). They specialise in these commodities for reasons of nature, and also for reasons of history. Many primary producing developing countries today were once colonies of developed countries that were used as suppliers of raw materials, and the processing of the primary commodities *in situ* was forbidden or discouraged (see later). The static gains from this pattern of specialisation may be offset by 'dynamic' losses (in a relative sense compared to other countries). Not even the static gains may be that large. Dowrick (1997), in a survey of trade and growth, makes the point that although there are theoretical reasons why trade liberalisation should increase welfare, 'it has proved rather more difficult to come up with good reasons why such welfare gains should be sizeable'. He quotes typical estimates of the benefits of trade liberalisation of about 1 per cent of GDP, and raises the question of whether a radical readjustment of an economy is worth such a small once-for-all gain. The answer must be 'no' if only static gains are on offer, with the prospect of future dynamic 'losses'. The case for trade liberalisation needs to be made on the basis of dynamic gains, but, as indicated above, some countries, pursuing static comparative advantage, may get locked into a productive structure of low growth activities.

This is why trade liberalisation needs to be combined, at the very least, with a trade strategy which seeks out new (dynamic) areas of comparative advantage, or promotes 'self-discovery' to use the terminology of Hausmann and Rodrik (2003) (see later). Trade liberalisation should not be regarded as an end in itself or as a substitute for a development strategy.

The second point to emphasise about the comparative cost doctrine is that the welfare gains from trade rest on the assumption of continuous full employment and balanced trade in the process of resource reallocation. In the above example of Portugal specialising in wine and England in cloth, the free trade doctrine assumes that all cloth workers in Portugal can find work in wine-making, and all wine-workers in England can find work in the cloth industry. If this is not the case, then the resource gains from specialisation will be offset by welfare losses from the unemployment of resources. Indeed, if countries have unemployed resources, the whole doctrine of comparative advantage based on the concept of opportunity cost loses meaning, because when unemployment exists the opportunity cost of using resources is zero. A contemporary example would be what is happening to farmers in Mexico who cannot compete with the United States (US) maize growers under the terms of the North American Free Trade Agreement (NAFTA) signed in 1994. They lose their jobs and have no alternative employment. US producers, and Mexican consumers, gain; Mexican farm workers lose (who also consume less of other products), and an absolute loss of welfare is possible. It was unemployment (combined with the free movement of capital) in the 1930s that convinced Keynes that free trade between countries is not necessarily optimal. In 1933, he published two articles, in the *New Statesman* and *Nation* (8 and 13 July) entitled 'National Self Sufficiency' in which he argued 'let goods be homespun' and 'finance be primarily national'. In conditions of unemployment, the economic benefit of national self-sufficiency for a country can outweigh the costs. Sir John Hicks also recounts (Hicks, 1959) how unemployment in the interwar years undermined his belief in free trade:

> The main thing that caused so much liberal opinion in England to lose faith in free trade was the helplessness of older liberalism in the face of massive unemployment, and the possibility of using import restrictions as an element in an active programme of fighting unemployment. One, of course, is obliged to associate this line of thought with the name of Keynes. It was this, almost alone, which led Keynes to abandon his early belief in Free Trade. (p. 48)

One of the major causes of unemployment is the inability of countries to grow in line with their productive potential because of balance of payments difficulties. There is nothing in the doctrine of comparative advantage that guarantees balanced trade. Ricardo recognised this full well and relied on the gold standard mechanism to produce an equilibrium with the relative prices of goods rising in surplus countries with gold inflows and falling in deficit countries with gold outflows. But the international gold standard never worked that way (Thirlwall, 2003), as Keynes (1936) recognised in his *General Theory* in defending the doctrine of mercantilism. In practice, surplus countries had low interest rates which stimulated investment and growth, while deficit countries had higher interest rates leading to unemployment. What adjusted the balance of trade was changes in income (output) not relative prices (see also Harrod, 1933). Those worried today about the unemployment and balance of payments consequences of globalisation may find some of Keynes's arguments prescient and worth revisiting (see also Stiglitz, 2002).

In 1848, John Stuart Mill published his *Principles of Political Economy* which reiterated Adam Smith's point about trade widening the market for goods, thereby permitting the division of labour: 'A country which produces for a larger market than its own can introduce a more extended division of labour, can make greater use of machinery, and is more likely to make inventions and improvements in the process of production'. Mill also stressed the role of trade as a conduit for the international dissemination of ideas and technology. There are three main forces at work here. Firstly, a domestic buyer of an imported good may imitate the production technique, or adapt the new technique if it is patented. Secondly, there may be a direct exchange of ideas between importer and exporter. Thirdly, new imported goods may stimulate ideas for further varieties of goods which increase welfare. 'New' growth theory (or endogenous growth theory), which incorporates trade, as pioneered by Grossman and Helpman (1991a, 1991b), incorporates many of these original ideas of Mill. But Mill recognised that the growth effects of trade depend on what a country specialises in; whether natural resource activities or manufacturing industries. A country with abundant natural resources may find itself at a disadvantage because it is the production of industrial goods, and particularly research-intensive goods, that produces technical dynamism. This is one aspect of what is now called in the economic development literature 'the curse of natural resources' which has been documented, among others, by Gylfason (2001) and Sachs and Warner (2001) who show that countries with 10 per cent more of their labour force engaged in primary production grow on average at 1 per cent less than other countries, controlling for differences in other country characteristics. One explanation is slower productivity growth in land-based activities combined with greater scope for rent-seeking behaviour and corruption, particularly when natural resources are in the hands of the State. The scenario is very different for countries specialising in industrial activities. In the 'new' growth theory models of Grossman and Helpman, referred to above, in which technical change is endogenous, trade affects growth by providing access to imported inputs and new ideas, and by increasing the size of the market. They show that trade *protection* can raise the long growth rate of an economy if it encourages investment in research-intensive activities in which a country has a comparative advantage. Protection will also keep expected profits higher than under free trade competition.

The neoclassical development of the doctrine of comparative advantage, associated with the names of two Swedish economists, Eli Heckscher (1919) and Bertil Ohlin (1933), attributes differences in relative costs of production not to differences in natural resources or levels of technology, but to differences in relative factor endowments, that is differences in the amount of capital per unit of labour. The Heckscher–Ohlin (H–O) theorem states that poor countries with an abundance of labour and scarce capital should find it relatively cheaper to produce and export labour-intensive goods, while richer countries with more capital and a relative shortage of labour should find it cheaper to produce and export capital-intensive commodities. This process should lead to greater wage equality in poor countries, and to greater inequality in richer countries. The link between trade and wages is through changes in product prices. This linkage, formalised by Stolper and Samuelson (1941), says that in poor countries the prices of labour-intensive products will rise, shifting resources to those sectors and raising the demand, and therefore wages, for unskilled labour. Contrariwise, the price of skill-intensive products will fall, reducing the demand for skilled labour and reducing wages. The opposite happens in rich countries, where the demand for unskilled labour falls, and the demand for skilled labour rises. A corollary of the Stolper–Samuelson (S–S) theorem is that protection increases the real wage of the scarce factor, because a tariff raises the price of import-competing goods, so that a reduction in protection will widen inequality in rich countries where unskilled labour is the scarce factor and reduce inequality in poor countries if it is skill-intensive activities that are protected the most. Samuelson (1948, 1949) later extended the S–S theorem to show rigorously how trade should equalise factor prices across countries, without any factor movements.[2]

On the surface, neoclassical theory is appealing and sounds plausible, but in practice some of the basic underlying assumptions of the model are weak, and the empirical evidence does not support it. The wage gap between unskilled and skilled labour in poor countries has not narrowed with the process of trade liberalisation (see later, Chapter 4), and the wage gap between rich and poor countries has not narrowed through time – if anything, it has increased. The weakest assumption of all is that technology is the same across countries. But if the productivity of labour is lower in poor countries than in rich countries, abundant labour in poor countries is not necessarily cheap labour in an economic sense. The money wage may be lower, but what determines the economic cost of labour is the efficiency wage or the wage cost per unit of output (wL/Y), which is the money wage (w) relative to labour productivity (Y/L). This consideration is one of the major explanations of what is called the Leontief Paradox, named after Wassily Leontief (1953) who first discovered that, contrary to the prediction of the Heckscher–Ohlin theorem, US exports were relatively labour-intensive compared to import substitutes.[3]

A major factor explaining differences in the level of labour productivity between countries is differences in the amount of human capital embodied in labour in the form of education and skill training. Trade will not equalise factor prices if the efficiency wage is lower in rich countries than in poor countries. A second point to bear in mind is that the theorem takes only two groups of countries – poor developing countries and rich developed countries – but when a poor country liberalises its trade, it will export and import more to and from both developed *and* other developing countries. As the demand for labour-intensive exports from poor countries rises in developed countries, wages in poor countries may rise, but may fall as a result of competitive imports from other poor developing countries. Mexico, for example, benefits from exporting labour-intensive products to the US, but now suffers from labour-intensive imports from China. What happens to the wages of unskilled labour in poor countries is the outcome of a balance of forces. Finally, the Heckscher–Ohlin theorem ignores the effect of long-term capital movements between countries, and particularly the impact of multinational investment in poor countries. When trade is freed, it tends to stimulate the flow of foreign direct investment to developing countries which adds to the demand for skilled, as well as unskilled, labour. If the demand for skilled labour rises by more (relative to the supply), this will increase the wages of skilled relative to unskilled labour in poor countries, also defying the predictions of the Heckscher–Ohlin model. As we shall see in Chapter 4, income and wage inequality is increasing in both rich and poor countries, driven by technological progress and trade which demands skilled labour.

Free Trade Enthusiasm in the Modern Era

Despite the putative arguments for free trade laid down by classical and neoclassical economic theory it was never seriously practised by countries (except by Britain post-1850) until after the Second World War with the establishment of the General Agreement on Tariffs and Trade (GATT) in 1947 and the general commitment by developed countries to the freeing of international trade in the wake of the protectionism and 'beggar-thy-neighbour' policies practised in the inter-war depression years. Even so, the process of trade liberalisation took a long time to gather momentum. Many developed countries maintained quite high tariff levels, and non-tariff barriers, until the early 1970s, and many developing countries, freed from their colonial past, went down the protectionist route, particularly in Latin America and parts of South Asia. It is only in the last 30 years or so that both developed and developing countries have made concerted efforts to liberalise trade between themselves, under pressure from a variety of sources. Dornbusch (1992) identifies four major pressures on developing countries: (i) the intellectual swing in favour of free markets; (ii) institutional pressures from the World Trade Organization (the successor to GATT) established in 1995, the World Bank, the IMF and other international organisations; (iii) greater awareness of the efficiency losses from restricting trade; and (iv) the alleged, or apparent, poor economic performance of countries pursuing protection.

The tide of opinion in favour of free markets had its intellectual roots in the ideas of economists such as Friedrich Von Hayek (1949) and Milton Friedman (1990), and gathered pace with the disillusion with planning, particularly as practised by the former Soviet Union and Eastern European countries. The role of the State in economic affairs came under increased scrutiny by both economic theoreticians and practitioners alike. Anti-statism became the fashion, and in the international arena it led to the development of the so-called Washington Consensus – a term originally coined by John Williamson of the Institute for International Economics in 1989 to refer to an agenda of desirable economic reforms in Latin America (see Williamson, 1993). The reforms quickly came to be seen as a model for the wider developing world, and was already embodied in the thinking of the World Bank and IMF.

The Washington Consensus extols the virtues of free markets and free trade for the achievement of more rapid economic progress, and includes among its major objectives: the privatisation of State enterprises; trade liberalisation, particularly the replacement of quantitative restrictions on trade with low and uniform tariffs, and openness to foreign direct investment. This is the route down which most developing countries have now gone. The institutional pressure from the World Bank and IMF for trade reform is well summarised in a direct quote from the IMF itself which states that the main goal of IMF-supported programmes in developing countries has been 'to improve the economic efficiency by creating a transparent and neutral system of incentives that eliminates anti-export bias, direct impediments to trade, and economic distortions caused by the trade regime' (IMF, 1998).

The greater awareness of the efficiency losses from restricting trade came from major empirical studies across countries sponsored by the Organisation for Economic Co-operation and Development (OECD) and the National Bureau of Economic and Social Research in the US showing the apparent wastefulness of import substitution regimes (see, for example, Little, et al., 1970; and summaries of this and other studies by Bhagwati, 1978 and Krueger, 1978). The East Asian experience of an outward-oriented development strategy based on exports, rather than a trade policy based on import substitution, was also regarded as salutary. Interestingly, however, economic success linked to export performance has not always been based on free trade and *laissez-faire*. It is true that the economies of Japan, South Korea, Taiwan, Singapore, Hong Kong, Malaysia, Indonesia and Thailand have recorded some of the highest export growth rates in the world since 1965 (averaging over 10 per cent per annum) and some of the highest GDP growth rates (averaging nearly 6 per cent per annum), but some of these countries have been very interventionist pursuing export promotion and import substitution at the same time. Japan and South Korea are clear examples, not to mention, today, modern China which is far removed from a *laissez-faire*, free trade economy, but which has the fastest rate of growth of exports and GDP in the world. China pursues an independent development strategy sometimes called the 'Beijing Consensus' (in contrast to the Washington Consensus), which makes it cautious about free trade and the free movement of international capital, although not about attracting long-term foreign direct investment. China is fortunate to be large enough (and stable enough) to plough its own furrow. Many developing countries, unfortunately, are either too small and vulnerable or too unstable to resist the orthodoxy because they are dependent on loan support from the IMF and World Bank.

The premise of poor economic performance of developing countries under protective trade regimes, as a motive for liberalisation, is not factually accurate. After the Second World War, while the developed countries started to dismantle tariffs and non-tariff barriers to trade under the auspices of GATT, the developing countries were allowed considerable 'policy space' and made no firm commitments to free trade. During the period from 1950 to 1979, the developing countries had their best economic performance in recent economic history (Chang, 2002). During colonialism, Asia and Africa grew extremely slowly, but in the post-colonial era until 1979 average per capita income grew at 3 per cent per annum, more than double that achieved by developed countries in the 19th century during their development process. Not all the success achieved during this period can be attributed, of course, to trade protection, but it is significant that in the period of neo-liberalism post-1980 the growth performance of many developing countries, particularly in Africa and Latin America, has been worse than in the pre-liberalisation era. In Africa as a whole, between 1980 and 2000, living standards actually fell, and per capita income growth in Latin America has averaged only 1.5 per cent per annum. Trade liberalisation has not delivered the performance promised by its advocates. As Rodrik (2004) says of Latin America:

> Latin America [during the 1990s] grew more slowly not only compared with other parts of the world – but also

compared to its own performance in the 1960s and 1970s. That is a *striking* empirical fact, the importance of which is hard to downplay. After all, Latin America of the 1960s and the 1970s is a region of import substitution, macro-economic populism, and protectionism, while Latin America of the 1990s is a region of openness, privatisation and liberalisation. The cold fact is that per capita economic growth performance has been abysmal during the 1990s by any standards. (p. 3)

The Case for Protection

Having rehearsed the orthodox arguments for free trade, and highlighted the recent political, institutional pressures on developing countries to embrace trade liberalisation (sometimes on spurious grounds), it is now time to give equal weight to the perfectly respectable economic arguments for protection, and then to look at the historical experience of countries now developed. Did they gain their industrial strength and economic power on the basis of free trade or protection? There is an interesting story to tell.

The first point to make is that for free trade in goods and services to maximise social welfare it needs to be shown, or proved, that the demand curve for goods measures the true social benefit of production and that the supply curve measures the true social cost. If this is the case, a restriction on trade, in the form of a tariff for example, will cause production and consumption distortions which reduce welfare, as illustrated in Figure 1.1.

DD and *SS* represent the domestic demand and supply of the good, respectively. *Pw* is the world

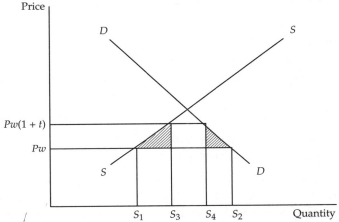

Figure 1.1   Production and consumption distortions from a tariff

price of the good, and S_1S_2 represents import demand at world prices to fill the gap between domestic demand and supply. Now suppose a percentage tariff (t) is imposed on the good raising the price to $Pw(1 + t)$. This produces two distortions: firstly, a production distortion, or loss of producer surplus, measured by the shaded area under the supply curve, because costs have risen; and secondly a consumption distortion, or loss of consumer surplus, measured by the shaded area under the demand curve, because prices have risen. These shaded areas under the supply and demand curves representing losses of producer and consumer surplus are often called Harberger triangles (Harberger, 1954) named after the distinguished Chicago economist Arnold Harberger. If the supply and demand curves, however, do not represent the true social cost and benefit of production and consumption, the loss of producer and consumer surplus from restricting trade and increasing domestic output may be exaggerated. In particular, the producer surplus (which is lost) may not properly measure the benefits of producing a good domestically because of various domestic distortions and market failures, such as positive externalities and technological spillovers from one industry to another or the existence of unemployment. In fact it is perfectly possible for the marginal social benefit from protecting industry, and increasing domestic production from S_1 to S_3 in Figure 1.1, to more than offset this loss of consumer and producer surplus. Harry Johnson (1964) identifies four major distortions particularly in the context of developing countries which constitute an *economic* argument for protection (so a country's real income will be above what it would otherwise be), although not necessarily an argument for tariffs if the distortions are domestic (see later):

1. *The infant industry argument for protection*: allowing industries to reach their optimum size in terms of average costs of production, so that they can compete with foreign competition in domestic and foreign markets. This argument goes back at least to Mill's *Principles of Political Economy* (1848), and to the writings of the German economist Friedrich List (1789–1846) in the 1840s. Mill promoted the idea of temporary infant industry

protection to stimulate industry. He writes: 'the only case in which, on mere principles of political economy, protecting duties can be defensible, is when they are imposed temporarily . . . in the hope of naturalizing a foreign industry'.[4] For List, infant industry protection was just one of a series of measures recommended for the industrial development of countries, recognising that economic development requires a combination of capital accumulation, technical progress and learning capabilities from both home and abroad. List was not the ardent protectionist that neo-liberals claim (Sai-wing Ho, 2005); he had a much broader vision of the growth and development process, and argued, in fact, that protection should be very selective: 'it should attempt to stimulate only those industries which have an assured home market and appear to have the best chance of success'. List anticipated the idea made rigorous by Krugman (1984) of 'import protection as export promotion' because a large domestic market, in the presence of economies of scale and decreasing costs, makes exports more competitive. Turning back to Figure 1.1, the supply curve there is drawn upward sloping representing an increase in the cost of producing additional units of output, whereas if there are economies of scale, and fixed costs can be spread over a larger volume of output, costs will fall and the supply curve will be downward sloping. There is no loss of producer surplus, but a gain. In recent times economists such as Stiglitz (2006) and Chang (2002) have argued forcibly and persuasively that developing countries need to protect themselves to switch their productive structure from reliance on primary production to the production of manufactured goods. Stiglitz argues not just for infant industry protection but infant *economy* protection. In other words, it may be better to impose a uniform tariff on *all* manufactured good imports to give time for an infant economy to establish a manufacturing base. This avoids the 'rent-seeking' behaviour of special interest groups that lobby for preferential protection for their own industry, and at the same time provides revenue for governments to spend for development purposes such as infrastructure, education and health. Stiglitz (2006) puts the simple but enduring case for protection very well when he writes:

> Without protection, a country whose static comparative advantage lies in, say agriculture, risks stagnation; its comparative advantage will remain in agriculture, with limited growth prospects. Broad based industrial protection can lead to an increase in the size of the industrial sector which is, almost everywhere, the source of innovation; many of these advances spill over into the rest of the economy, as do the benefits from the development of institutions, like financial markets, that accompany the growth of an industrial sector. Moreover, a large and growing industrial sector (and the tariffs on manufactured goods) provide revenues with which the government can fund education, infrastructure, and other ingredients necessary for broad-based growth. (p. 72)

In fact, the effect on imports of uniform revenue-raising tariffs on all industrial imports would be little different from an equivalent depreciation of the currency or temporary industrial subsidies – but with the latter policies there would be no revenue.

Chang (2002), in his famous book *Kicking Away the Ladder* (evocative words taken from List) reminds us of the historical experience of the now developed countries (see below), and the time it takes for industries to reach their most efficient scale to compete both domestically, with foreign competition, and internationally, because learning and absorption of technology is a gradual process. Before the Second World War, the comparative advantage of Japan and South Korea was in rice production, yet today these countries have two of the most successful steel industries in the world, based not on free trade but protection over a number of years. The examples could be multiplied; on the other hand, protection can go wrong. Inappropriate industries may be chosen, or protection be granted for too long so that the infant industries never grow up. The conditions for success are firstly that the choice of infant industries needs to be realistic; secondly that infant industry protection needs to be combined with an export strategy in order to provide the foreign exchange to pay for imported inputs and to widen the market; and thirdly that the 'rent-seeking' activities of government officials and politicians made possible by protective policies need to be controlled (as Stiglitz's proposal would do). Anne Krueger (1997), an ardent free-trader, argues that it is impossible to identify infant industries, but the facts and history are against her. But, in any case, even if the infant industries are relatively inefficient, it may be more beneficial for an economy to have some industry than no industry at all because of knowledge externalities and spillovers that in recent years have been highlighted by so-called 'new trade theory' (see below). Krueger (1998) further claims that the traditional infant industry argument of dynamic gains outweighing static losses 'has now been overturned'. This is simply not true.

2.   *The externalities argument for protection*: where the social benefit of increased domestic production is greater than the private benefit due to spillovers. There are both micro and macro considerations (Ocampo and Taylor, 1998), both relating to productivity effects. In a free market, resources may not shift naturally or easily from low-return to high-return sectors of an economy because of barriers to mobility. If the manufacturing sector is the major source of productivity growth in the early stages of development, because it is an increasing returns activity, promoting industry, or not protecting it, has implications for the growth of the whole economy. At the micro level there are the technological spillovers from one industry to another to consider, arising from research and development (R&D), knowledge creation, learning by doing and the production of skilled labour. Without the protection of industry, a substantial source of productivity growth may be lost.

These considerations are the foundations of 'new trade theory', pioneered by Krugman (1986) and Grossman and Helpman (1991b) in the 1980s and 1990s, which uses increasing returns and imperfect competition to explain why large spatial differences in economic development exist within and between countries, when orthodox trade theory predicts convergence. It is essentially the division of labour, or specialisation, that leads to increasing returns and the concentration of manufacturing in particular geographic locations which then generates externalities, both pecuniary and technological. In addition, with knowledge spillovers from innovating to following firms, new trade theory extends the infant industry argument to protecting not only industries, but the process of innovation itself. Grossman and Helpman (1991b) show how trade liberalisation can have negative effects on R&D by displacing innovative activities. Without protection, countries will tend to specialise in low-technology products. Trade restrictions give the opportunity for countries to develop a more complex, sophisticated, interconnected industrial base. This is what the historical evidence shows. All this means that *if* there is a short-term cost of protecting infant industries,[5] it is outweighed by the long-term gains from a more dynamic industrial structure. As in 'new growth theory', which endogenises technical change, protection will promote growth if the forces of comparative advantage push resources towards activities with superior growth potential; that is activities that promote R&D, innovate and produce goods higher up the value chain. Despite the logic of the argument, however, the pioneers of new trade theory have been reluctant to endorse protection; witness, for example, the remarkable claim by Krugman (1993a) that 'by emphasising the virtues of free trade, we also emphasise our intellectual superiority over the unenlightened who do not understand comparative advantage'. The fear of protection seems to be rent-seeking behaviour and that governments lack the necessary information for optimal policy intervention. To quote Krugman (1987) again: 'Free trade rules are best for a world whose politics are as imperfect as its markets'. However, this did not stop many countries in South East Asia adopting remarkably successful strategic industrial and trade strategies which have propelled them into industrial giants to challenge the manufacturing base of Europe and North America. Perhaps it is these countries that Krugman (1987) had in mind when he also declared 'free trade is not *passé* but it is an idea that has irretrievably lost its innocence . . . it can never be asserted as the policy that economic theory tells us is always right'.

3.   *The domestic distortion argument for protection*: for example, in the labour market where the social cost of using labour is less than the private cost because of unemployment. This is a classic argument for intervention that goes back to Adam Smith.[6] Poor developing countries have pervasive unemployment, so that the social (opportunity)

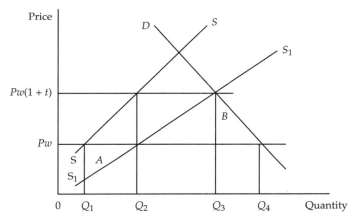

Figure 1.2 Protection when social cost of labour is less than the private cost

cost of using labour is less than the private cost (the wage). The argument is illustrated in Figure 1.2, which is a modification of Figure 1.1.

S_1S_1 is the social cost of production, and SS is the private cost of production (as before) which is t per cent above the social cost. Under free trade, domestic producers will produce up to Q_1 where the private cost equals the world price of the good, Pw. Demand is Q_4, so Q_1Q_4 will be imported. Q_1Q_2 imports could be replaced, however, by additional domestic production Q_1Q_2, with real savings equal to the area A, if domestic producers are either offered tariff protection which brings the domestic price to $Pw(1 + t)$, or a subsidy of t per cent which reduces the private cost to the social cost. It can be seen immediately in the example, however, that the welfare effects of tariffs and subsidies are not the same. In the case of a tariff, t, the price of the good rises and there is a loss of consumer surplus, *B*, which may be greater than the welfare gain of *A*. In the case of a subsidy, however, there is no loss of consumer surplus, and the welfare gain is unequivocal. In this respect, a subsidy to labour is first best (see later).

4. *The optimal tariff argument for protection*: where international distortions cause the domestic rate of transformation between goods to diverge from the foreign rate of transformation due, for example, to monopoly power in international trade, so that if a country is a big buyer, it can turn the terms of trade in its favour by restricting imports. This gain could be in excess of the efficiency loss from the production and consumption distortions from a tariff illustrated in Figure 1.1. The argument goes back at least to Robert Torrens (1833). In practice, the optimum tariff argument is not a serious one for developing countries because they are not big enough buyers of products individually. But there is another terms of trade argument, and that is that the price of primary commodities relative to industrial goods has been falling by at least 1 per cent per annum on average for the last 100 years or more (see Cashin and McDermott, 2002). This represents a substantial real income loss for countries specialising in the production and export of primary commodities. If trade liberalisation reinforces traditional patterns of specialisation, the real income loss for poor developing countries is perpetuated. There is a case for protection to alter the structure of production in favour of commodi-

ties that have more favourable terms of trade in world markets. This was one of the major arguments originally made by Prebisch, as discussed earlier, in advocating import substitution policies in Latin America. The avoidance of terms of trade loss may offset the costs of protection.[7]

Another economic argument for protection, not considered by orthodox theory, is the balance of payments argument. Johnson (1964) calls this argument a 'non-argument' (like the terms of trade argument) because of the classical/neoclassical presumption that the balance of payments is self-adjusting through relative price, or exchange rate, changes. If trade liberalisation, however, causes the balance of payments to deteriorate because imports rise faster than exports, and it is income that falls to restore balance of payments equilibrium (not relative price changes), the real resource gains from trade may be offset by the welfare losses from the underutilisation of domestic resources. In other words, if trade liberalisation leads to balance of payments problems which cause unemployment, the social cost of labour is less than the private cost of labour, and we have seen above that in these circumstances there is a legitimate economic argument for protection. We will examine in Chapter 2 the evidence on the balance of payments consequences of trade liberalisation. Interestingly, Article XVIII of GATT allowed member countries to temporarily restrict trade in goods and services for balance of payments purposes, just as there was a 'scarce currency' clause in the Articles of

Agreement of the IMF that would have allowed countries to discriminate against goods from countries in balance of payments surplus – but the clause has never been used.

Despite the body of trade theory which legitimises protection, Dani Rodrik (1988), the well known trade and development economist from Harvard, is correct that the arguments have still not penetrated the vast literature on trade policy in developing countries which continue to reflect the orthodox view that trade liberalisation is optimal, as if written in tablets of stone. Yet, as Rodrik says, the market imperfections of the type analysed above would appear, if anything, to be more prevalent and serious in developing countries than in developed countries. One of the most ardent exponents and advocates of the free trade doctrine, even for developing countries, is the distinguished trade theorist Jagdish Bhagwati. Krugman says of Bhagwati (in Subramanian, 2005) it is he, above all else, who has played a 'large if subtle role in keeping protectionism from becoming respectable'.

Bhagwati's Lament

In his polemical book, *Free Trade Today*, Bhagwati (2001) bemoans (unnecessarily) the lack of economists willing to put the argument for free trade. He recognises many of the distortions discussed above, but is adamant that they should be tackled domestically rather than through trade restrictions. Indeed, it was Bhagwati and Ramaswami (1963) who first showed rigorously how domestic market distortions are not an argument against free trade, but for correcting the distortions directly. In the labour market, if the social cost of labour is less than the private cost, the first-best policy is a wage subsidy plus free trade, as we saw in Figure 1.2. In the product market, if there is a production externality, the first-best policy would be a production subsidy plus free trade. In the case of international distortions, such as monopoly power in trade, where a country's terms of trade depend on its volume of trade, the optimum tariff argument applies, and this is the first-best policy – but this is the only case for tariffs that Bhagwati concedes. He is also concerned with the 'directly unproductive profit-seeking activities (DUP)' (a phrase coined by him) which arise when tariffs, quotas and licenses are used to control trade (see also, Tullock, 1967). These need to be taken seriously, but should not be exaggerated. As Ocampo and Taylor (1998) say, 'if quotas cover only a fraction of imports, and imports are a fraction of GDP, associated rents and rent seeking outlays cannot be huge'. Moreover, if there is not full employment, or the balance of payments is a constraint on growth, the additional income flows associated with a larger volume of domestic output by the imposition of import controls will generate welfare gains. It is also possible that rents in the right hands may be invested productively and not consumed.

If subsidies to labour and production are first best when market imperfections and distortions are domestic, and protection is second best, the issue arises of how subsidies are financed. If they are financed by taxes on wage income and profits, this adds further distortions in an economy. In practice, a large fraction of tax revenue in developing countries is raised from trade taxes. Tariffs are being used to pay subsidies. Reducing trade taxes, to make trade freer, may seriously undermine a country's fiscal position and make it more difficult to pursue desirable domestic policies to promote development which are also welfare enhancing. This is where issues of the distribution of income and consumption become important to consider. The welfare effects of imposing tariffs on necessary consumption goods for the poor, and on necessary inputs for industrial development, are not the same as the imposition of tariffs or quotas on luxury consumption goods for the rich. Bhagwati's plea for greater freedom of trade is silent on these distributional issues.

Indeed, none of Bhagwati's attempted rehabilitations of free trade address directly the important issues of infant industry protection, the need for structural change in poor countries, or the distributional consequences of trade liberalisation and its effects on the poor (see later for the evidence). On the other hand, he is honest when he makes the important distinction between the effect of trade on *current welfare* on the one hand, and the effect of trade on *growth* on the other; they are not the same.

In most standard growth models, the effect of trade on growth is ambiguous. In the Harrod growth model, for example (see Thirlwall, 2002), free trade may reduce the capital–output ratio, raising growth; but may also reduce the savings ratio, reducing growth. In the neoclassical Solow model (1956), trade cannot affect the steady-state growth rate, although it can be altered if the steady state is not treated as an exogenous constant. Only in the 'new' growth theories of Grossman and Helpman (1991a, 1991b) does trade have the potential to raise the growth rate permanently through learning and spillover effects, but only if they are continuous. Bhagwati remarks, interestingly:

> Those who assert that free trade will . . . lead necessarily to greater growth *either* are ignorant of the fine-nuances of the theory and the vast quantity of literature to the contrary on the subject at hand *or* are nonetheless basing their argument on a different premise; that is, that the preponderant evidence on the issue (in the post-war period) suggests that freer trade tends to lead to greater growth after all. In fact, where theory includes several models that can lead in different directions, the policy economist is challenged to choose the model that is most appropriate to the reality she confronts. And I would argue that, in the present instance, we must choose the approaches that generate favourable outcomes for growth when trade is liberalised. (pp. 42–3)

In Chapter 2 we shall examine the evidence on the relationship between trade liberalisation and economic growth, but first it is useful and salutary to look at the experience of the now-developed countries to see whether they developed on the basis of free trade or protection. Unfortunately for the free trade doctrine, it is the latter that turns out to be the case, so the developed countries (and international institutions) that preach free trade to developing countries are preaching what they never practised themselves.

Protection in Historical Perspective

The best historical description of the role of protection in the early industrialisation phase of the now-developed countries is given by Ha-Joon Chang, the Cambridge economist, in three fascinating books: *Kicking Away the Ladder: Development Strategy in Historical Perspective* (2002); *Why Developing Countries Need Tariffs?* (2005); and *Bad Samaritans: Rich Nations, Poor Policies and the Threat to the Developing World* (2007). In this section we rely heavily on the evidence in these books.[8]

The current developed countries of the world, including Britain, the United States and the countries of continental Europe and Scandinavia did not develop their economies on the basis of free trade. On the contrary, they heavily protected their domestic industries, and also did their utmost to prevent the countries that they colonised from competing with them. Britain started to protect and foster industries as early as the late 15th century when Henry VII took the deliberate decision to challenge the successful woollen manufacturing industry of Belgium and Holland, which was reliant on the export of British wool. He taxed the export of raw wool and banned export of some types of unfinished cloth in order to encourage processing at home. Henry VIII continued the protectionist policy, and by the middle of the reign of Elizabeth I, Britain had sufficient processing capacity to ban the export of wool entirely, which ruined the cloth industry of the Low Countries. Britain first became rich on its woollen industry nurtured by the State. Serious protection of new manufacturing industries started with Robert Walpole in 1721, using tariffs, subsidies, tariff rebates on imported inputs and other protective devices – all of which are deemed to be damaging to developing countries today. In the early 19th century, Britain imposed some of the highest tariff rates on manufactured goods in the world, averaging 45–55 per cent.

Britain also prevented its colonies from producing manufactured goods. William Pitt the Elder, the British Prime Minister from 1766 to 1768, is quoted by Friedrich List (1885) as saying that 'the colonies should not be permitted to manufacture so much as a horsenail'. All sorts of devices were resorted to in the 18th century to keep the colonies as producers of primary commodities, giving subsidies to production, and reducing tariffs on raw material imports into Britain. A law passed in 1699 forbade the export of processed wool products from the English colonies, including Ireland. In 1700, all cotton goods from India were prohibited. In the 1720s, Walpole gave export subsidies and abolished import duties on raw materials produced in the American colonies so that their comparative advantage stayed in primary products. Some manufacturing activities were even prohibited, such as high value-added steel products in America. The use of tariffs by the colonies was either banned or, where used for revenue purposes, a tax was imposed on the industry concerned to neutralise its competitive advantage. In other countries not colonised by Britain, 'unequal treaties' were signed which took away the tariff autonomy of the countries and set 'binding' tariffs that countries could not exceed, typically about 5 per cent in countries such as Brazil, China, Japan, Siam (now Thailand) and Persia (now Iran). With regard to Europe, Britain also tried to protect itself against competition, although to less effect. The export of some types of machinery embodying new technology was banned, and for over sixty years from 1719 to 1782 there was a ban on the emigration of skilled labour from Britain. Those who defied the ban, and did not return within six months, had their possessions confiscated and citizenship withdrawn.

Britain's industrial revolution gathered momentum in the mid-18th century, when protection still prevailed. It would be a rewriting of history, therefore, to argue that Britain started its development process on the basis of free trade. Britain did not start dismantling its structure of protection until the repeal of the Corn Laws in 1846, but by then it had already attained technological superiority over all other countries in the world. From then on, Britain preached free trade, but as List (1885) remarked, such preaching was like 'kicking away the ladder' up which one has climbed oneself so that no-one else can reach the top. List comments:

> It is a very common clever device that where anyone has attained the summit of greatness, he kicks away the ladder by which he has climbed up, in order to deprive others of the means of climbing up after him. In this lies the secret of the cosmopolitan doctrine of Adam Smith, and the cosmopolitan tendencies of his great contemporary William Pitt, and of all his successors in the British Government administrations. Any nation which by means of protective duties and restrictions on navigation has raised her manufacturing power and her navigation to such a degree of development that no other nation can sustain free competition with her, can do nothing wiser than throw away these ladders of her greatness, to preach to other nations the benefits of free trade, and to declare in penitent tone that she has hitherto wandered in the paths of error, and has now for the first time succeeded in discovering the truth. (pp. 295–6)

The United States followed Britain's protectionist route at the end of the 18th century, contrary to Adam Smith's advice in the *Wealth of Nations*. Here is what Smith had to say:

> Were the Americans, either by combination or by any other sort of violence to stop the importation of European manufactures, and, by thus giving a monopoly to such of their own countrymen as could manufacture the like goods, divert any considerable part of their capital into this employment, they would retard instead of accelerating the further increase in the value of their annual produce, and would obstruct instead of promoting the progress of their country towards real wealth and greatness. (pp. 347–8)

If the United States had followed Adam Smith's advice, it would have remained an economic backwater for a long time, instead of becoming the richest industrialised country in the world. In the 19th century, the US economy was the fastest growing in the world, and also the most protectionist. Paul Bairoch (1993) has described the United States as 'the mother country and bastion of modern protectionism'. It was the US Treasury Secretary, Alexander Hamilton in 1791, who first coined the term 'infant industry', and who first argued the case for industrialisation by protection using tariffs, subsidies and other means, recognising that without protection it would be impossible for America to compete against more advanced countries, notably Britain. List, in his classic book *The National System of Political Economy*, first published in German in 1841, claims that he first learnt the infant industry argument for protection while in exile in the US in the 1820s. The US first imposed tariffs on industrial goods in 1789. Protection continued to increase in the 19th century and by 1870, import tariffs accounted for more than 50 per cent of the value of imports. Protection continued in the early 20th century, and was even strengthened in the 1930s with the 'Smoot–Hawley' tariff which raised the average tariff on manufactured goods to nearly 50 per cent. According to Bairoch (1993) no other country implemented a more protectionist policy to promote its industry than the United States. Only after the Second World War did it start to liberalise its trade, having already established industrial supremacy, and was able to 'kick away the ladder', as Britain had done a century earlier.

German industrial policy in the 19th century was heavily influenced by the views of List. He believed that import duties should not only be used to protect industry but also to promote it, supported by the State. Germany's average tariff rate on industrial goods was not as high as in the US, but the German State actively promoted industry by 'assigning monopoly rights, establishing industrial cartels, providing export subsidies, importing industrial experts and skilled labour, establishing large banks and making large investments in coal production and railway and road construction' (Skarstein, 2007).

Japan was prevented from using tariffs up to 1911 because of the 'unequal treaties' signed, as referred to earlier. But after 1911, Japan embarked on a comprehensive development strategy, a major part of which included substantial tariff protection, combined with subsidies to key (infant) industries and State investment in infrastructure. Just before the First World War, Japan's average tariff on manufactured imports was 30 per cent. The protectionist stance continued after the Second World War, with tariffs on car imports, for example, of nearly 40 per cent. Protectionism in the 1950s and 1960s was combined with the highest GDP growth rate of any country in the world. If Japan had listened to the free-traders, it would have no industrial base.

The average tariff rates on manufactured goods for selected developed countries in their early stages of development are shown in Table 1.1.

Table 1.1   *Average tariff rates on manufactured products*
for selected developed countries in their early
stages of development (weighted average, in
percentages of value)[1]

Country	1820[2]	1875[2]	1913	1925	1931	1950
Austria[3]	R	15–20	18	16	24	18
Belgium[4]	6–8	9–10	9	15	14	11
Denmark	25–35	15–20	14	10	n.a.	3
France	R	12–15	20	21	30	18
Germany[5]	8–12	4–6	13	20	21	26
Italy	n.a.	8–10	18	22	46	25
Japan[6]	R	5	30	n.a.	n.a.	n.a.
Netherlands[4]	6–8	3–5	4	6	n.a.	11
Russia	R	15–20	84	R	R	R
Spain	R	15–20	41	41	63	n.a.
Sweden	R	3–5	20	16	21	9
Switzerland	8–12	4–6	9	14	19	n.a.
UK	45–55	0	0	5	n.a.	23
US	35–45	40–50	44	37	48	14

Notes:

R = Numerous and important restrictions on
    manufactured imports and therefore average tariff rates
    are not meaningful.
1. World Bank (1991, p. 97, Box table 5.2) provides a
   similar table, but the figures are *unweighted* averages.
2. These are very approximate rates, and give range of
   average rates, not extremes.
3. Austria-Hungary before 1925.
4. In 1820, Belgium was united with the Netherlands.
5. The 1820 figure is for Prussia only.
6. Before 1911, Japan was obliged to keep low tariff rates
   (up to 5 per cent) through a series of 'unequal treaties'
   with the European countries and the USA.

Source: Chang (2002).

Notice the very high tariff rates for the UK and US in 1820, the continued high rates in the US up to 1950, and the relatively high rates in France, Germany and Italy too. These are much higher rates that the average nominal tariff on imports of manufactures into today's developing countries.

Average tariff rates for developed countries fell dramatically after 1950, but it is interesting to note that five of the six fastest growing countries during the 'golden age' of growth 1950–73 were still the highest tariff countries: Japan (8.05 per cent), Italy (4.95 per cent), Austria (4.90 per cent), Finland (4.25 per cent) and France (4.05 per cent). Germany was the only fast growing country in this period with the lowest tariffs.

The historical record tells the same story. O'Rourke (2000) takes ten of today's developed countries over the period 1875–1914 and shows a positive relation between tariff rates and GDP growth, controlling for other factors influencing growth. Clemens and Williamson (2001) examine 35 developed and developing countries over the period 1875–1908 and 1924–34 and also find a positive relation between the level of tariffs and growth. Vamvakidis (2002) takes the inter-war period 1920–40 and finds a positive relation between tariff rates and growth across 22 countries (although not for the period 1870–1910). Studies of more recent years show the same positive relation between levels of trade restrictions and growth, controlling for other variables. Yanikkaya (2003) takes more than 100 countries over the period

1970–97 and finds that both tariffs and export taxes seem to be associated with faster growth. He concludes: 'these results . . . provide support for the infant industry case for protection and for strategic trade policy'. And Rodrik (2001) asserts: 'cross national comparisons of the literature reveals no systematic relationship between a country's average level of tariff and non-tariff restrictions and its subsequent economic growth rate. If anything the evidence for the 1990s indicates a *positive* (but statistically insignificant) relationship between tariffs and economic growth' (italics in the original).

It can be said with some confidence that tariffs never harmed economic progress in the countries now developed. On the contrary, they 'climbed the ladder' on the back of tariffs and other protectionist devices. All we know is that as countries get richer they dismantle trade restrictions, not that they get richer *because* they liberalise trade. The issue for developing countries today is not whether to protect, but how to protect in order to ensure the dynamic efficiency of its nascent industrial activities.

The Measurement and Process of Trade Liberalisation

To measure the degree and process of trade liberalisation is not such an easy task as it may appear on the surface. There are many different measures of protection, and many different measures and concepts of trade liberalisation and trade openness. Here we will outline the main indicators that have been proposed in the literature on trade and development, and used in empirical work. Pritchett (1996) gives a comprehensive survey of the different measures of liberalisation and openness and concludes that no one measure is ideal, but more serious for economic analysis is that the most commonly used measures are not closely correlated with each other. The first thing to make clear, however, is that trade liberalisation is not the same as trade openness, and the two concepts should not be confused. This is the distinction that Dowrick and Golley (2004) make between 'revealed openness' and 'policy openness'. Trade (or 'revealed') openness is readily measured by the share of exports in GDP, by the share of imports in GDP, or by the share of total trade in GDP. This is clearly defined, but it does not say why some countries trade more than others. Are they highly specialised because of natural comparative advantage and a small home market, or because of 'policy openness', that is no trade barriers? For example, a country may have a high ratio of exports and imports to GDP because it has abundant natural resources which it can only export, and use the foreign exchange to pay for its import requirements, but may operate a very illiberal trade regime which makes trade difficult in other activities. Equally, a country with a low ratio of total trade may be quite liberal in its trading practices.

One way of coping with this difficulty is to take the difference between the actual ratio of total trade (exports plus imports) to GDP (the trade intensity ratio) and the ratio *predicted* on the basis of natural resource endowments and other factors such as distance to markets, quality of transport infrastructure, and so on. If the difference is positive the country can be classified as 'liberal' or 'open'; if the difference is negative, the country is classified as 'protected' or 'closed'. This is what Leamer (1988) does in a classic paper. This approach, however, implicitly assumes that trade barriers are the only omitted variables and are uncorrelated with the included variables to explain predicted trade openness. Leamer recognises this weakness and tries to overcome it by studying the pattern of residuals to detect other factors. Looking at the residuals commodity by commodity he identifies some interesting missing variables: tastes (Japan's coffee); omitted resources (Iceland's fish); historical accidents (Swiss watches). We like his conclusion at the end: diagnosis, he says, is an art, not a science!

The most common measure of trade liberalisation focuses on what is happening to tariffs and non-tariff barriers to trade; whether trade is biased against exports in favour of import substitution, and the general micro and macro environment of a country in which trade takes place including the level of the exchange rate; whether the State has a monopoly of major exports; whether there is free mobility of capital; the tax burden, and monetary and financial conditions.

Average tariff rates, export taxes, total taxes on international trade and indices of non-tariff barriers are all obvious measures of protection, but there are difficulties in using any one of these indices as a measure of trade liberalisation. For one thing a country may substitute one measure of protection for another. Non-tariff barriers, for example, may be reduced, but tariff rates raised to compensate, and vice versa. Secondly, nominal tariffs on goods are not the appropriate basis for assessing the restrictive effect of a tariff structure on trade. The nominal rate does not measure how inefficient (or costly) producers can be without incurring competition and losing market share. This is measured by the protection of value-added. This is the so-called *effective* rate of protection, a concept pioneered by Corden (1966). Since value-added is the difference between the value of output and inputs, not only is the tariff on output important when measuring the degree of protection, but also the tariff on inputs. Different countries may have the same nominal rates of protection on finished goods, but different levels of effective protection. Equally, the same nominal tariff cuts may mean different degrees of change in the effective rate of protection. A third point to make is that average tariff rates are often measured in empirical work by the ratio of tariff revenues to the values of imports, but this is not a measure of the official tariff rate, but of the collected rate. In the extreme, if a very high tariff discouraged imports completely, there would be no revenue, and the measured tariff rate would be zero!

More useful is to devise measures of trade regimes which can then be ranked from illiberal to liberal or from protectionist to liberalised, and to look at the various indices through time. Among the first studies to classify trade regimes in this way were those by Krueger (1978) and Bhagwati (1978), sponsored by the National Bureau of Economic Research. They focused on the extent to which the structure of protection and incentives is biased against exports. The degree of bias of the trade regime at time *t* is defined as:

$$B_t = \frac{EER_m}{EER_x} = \frac{E_m(1 + t + n + PR)}{E_x(1 + s + r)} \tag{1.1}$$

where EER_m and EER_x are the effective exchange rates of imports and exports, respectively; E_m is the nominal exchange rate for imports; t is the import tariff; n is other charges on imports; PR is the premium associated with quantitative restrictions on imports, such as licenses and quotas; E_x is the nominal exchange rate for exports; s is net subsidies on exports, and r is a measure of other incentives to exports. If $B_t > 1$, this implies that trade is biased against exports in favour of import substitutes. On this basis, trade liberalisation can be defined as any policies that reduce the degree of anti-export bias. In this sense, it is clear that a neutral trade regime does not imply the absence of tariffs and free trade. Equally, liberalised trade and open economies may still involve trade distortions and anti-export bias. Indeed in her empirical work, Krueger (1978) found that a reduction in bias, rather than trade liberalisation as such, was the most important factor affecting the export performance of countries.

An alternative way of defining the bias, and an easier way to measure (Krueger, 1998), is by the extent to which the ratio of the domestic price of import competing goods (P_{md}) to their international (world) price (P_{mw}), relative to the ratio of domestic price of importables (P_{xd}) compared to their international price (P_{xw}), deviates from unity; that is

$$B_t = \frac{P_{md}/P_{mw}}{P_{xd}/P_{xw}} \tag{1.2}$$

If $P_{mw}/P_{xw} = 1$, then if $P_{md}/P_{xd} > 1$, the trade regime is biased against exports in favour of import substitutes, and if $P_{md}/P_{xd} < 1$, the trade regime favours export promotion.

Greenaway et al. (1998), in their major study of trade liberalisation and growth using a panel of 73 countries, construct a similar index to Krueger's which also measures the relative distortion (D) of the price of exportables to importables. It is calculated as:

$$D = \frac{(1+t)}{(1+s)} \tag{1.3}$$

where t is the tariff on imports and s the rate of subsidy to exports. A ratio of unity implies trade neutrality; a ratio greater than unity implies anti-export bias in favour of import substitution, while a ratio less than unity implies an export-oriented trade strategy.

Michaely et al. (1991), in their study for the World Bank on liberalising trade in developing countries, define the process of trade liberalisation in a similar way to the measures constructed by Krueger and by Greenaway et al., namely: 'any change which leads to a country's trade system towards neutrality in the sense of bringing its economy close to the situation that would prevail if there was no government interference'. The authors construct their own index of country trade liberalisation on a scale from 1 to 20, from complete repression to fully liberalised.

David Greenaway (see Greenaway and Nam, 1988) was very influential in the World Bank classification of trade regimes in its *World Development Report 1987*. Four categories of countries were identified and 41 countries classified: (i) strongly outward-oriented countries where there are very few trade or foreign exchange controls, and trade and industrial policies do not discriminate between production for the home market and exports, and between purchases of domestic goods and foreign goods; (ii) moderately outward-oriented countries where the overall incentive structure is slightly biased towards the production of goods for the home market rather than for export, and favours the purchase of domestic goods; (iii) moderately inward-oriented countries, where there is a more definite bias against exports and in favour of import substitution; and (iv) strongly inward-oriented countries where trade controls and the incentive structure strongly favours production for the domestic market and discriminate against imports.

Many investigators and international organisations devise their own measures of protection and liberalisation, using multiple criteria. There is the Sachs and Warner (1995) Openness Index. Countries are classified as 'open' or 'closed' according to five criteria. A country is regarded as 'closed' if at least one of the criteria is satisfied: an average tariff rate higher than 40 per cent; non-tariff barriers covering more than 40 per cent of imports; a socialist economic system; a state monopoly of major exports, or a black market exchange rate premium in excess of 20 per cent. The criteria are arbitrary, of course, and the measure of 'openness' is crude, but nonetheless many investigators have used the index to classify countries, and to measure the timing of liberalisation.

Edwards (1992, 1998) uses nine different measures of openness: the Sachs–Warner openness index; the World Bank's 1987 trade classification; Leamer's (1988) openness index based on the average residuals from trade flow regressions; the average black market exchange rate premium; the average import tariff; the average coverage of non-tariff barriers; the Heritage Foundation index of distortions (see below); the ratio of total revenue from trade taxes to total trade, and

Wolf's (1993) regression-based index of import distortions in 1985. The relationship found between GDP growth and trade liberalisation often depends on the index used.

Since 1995 the Heritage Foundation in Washington has constructed an Index of Economic Freedom which considers a broad array of institutional factors, one of which is trade policies. A trade policy score of 1 to 5 is given to countries based on their average tariff rate, the extent of non-tariff barriers, and the degree of corruption in the customs service. Based on this trade policy grading scale, five broad levels of protection are distinguished: very low (free), low, moderate, high and very high (repressed). Countries can be classified according to category, and their economic performance analysed.

The process of trade liberalisation can take many different forms, but as Michaely et al. (1991) say, in their massive volume of case studies of trade liberalisation in developing countries, 'very little is known about essential attributes of a change from one [trade] regime to another; of a move away from a distorted trade policy regime towards a more neutral one'. On the other hand, we know that the issues of timing, phasing and sequencing are likely to be important in the design and implementation of a successful trade liberalisation policy.

Often the first stage of liberalisation is the dismantling of non-tariff barriers to trade in the form of quotas and licenses, not necessarily the reduction of tariffs. In fact, tariffs often rise to compensate for the removal of quantitative restrictions on imports. This makes protection more transparent and reduces rent-seeking behaviour. When protection is removed from an industry, production is likely to decline and unemployment rise. Capital is specific and will be left unutilised, and labour may not be mobile enough to be employed in other activities. This is a serious worry and can undermine the static welfare gains from trade liberalisation. It is certainly an argument against liberalising imports too rapidly. As the relative prices of factors of production and goods change, there is also likely to be considerable redistribution effects which need taking account of in the process of liberalisation (see Chapter 4).

The other big worry is the effect of trade liberalisation on the balance of payments. If imports rise faster than exports, balance of payments difficulties may arise, which have negative growth consequences. This has implications for the sequencing of trade liberalisation. Imports should not be liberalised before the export sector has had time to adjust or respond in order for foreign exchange to be available to meet the higher import bill. In terms of policy, it means that anti-export bias needs removing, or export subsidies given, before serious import liberalisation takes place (as was the case in Japan and South Korea, for example).

East Asia provides an interesting case study of how countries should proceed, where the process of trade liberalisation was gradual and export-oriented, in contrast to many Latin American countries where the process of liberalisation was sudden and no attention was paid to the sequencing. Sachs (1987) documents the East Asian and Latin American experience and concludes that it is only sensible and efficient to liberalise imports significantly once a sustained increase in exports, and structural change in favour of tradeables, has been achieved. Not only South Korea and Japan, but also Taiwan and Hong Kong all gave greater emphasis to export promotion than import liberalisation, which encouraged the domestic output of tradeables. By contrast, in the majority of Latin American countries, imports were liberalised without any regard to exports, or the creation of new productive capacity to compete with imports. On the contrary, many Latin American countries dismantled or cut back export promotion schemes whether or not they had been successful in the past. We shall look in more detail in Chapter 2 at the impact of trade liberalisation on export growth, import growth and the balance of payments of countries.

Another message from the experience of liberalisation is that liberalisation is much more likely to be successful in an environment of internal and external stability. It is particularly important not to allow the exchange rate to appreciate, which otherwise worsens the balance between export and import growth. This means that countries need to retain control of the capital account of the balance of payments, and not to liberalise capital flows at the same time as trade. Unfortunately, many Latin American countries, such as Mexico, Argentina and Peru, when they liberalised in the 1980s and early 1990s, allowed their exchange rate to appreciate which damaged the trade balance and impacted negatively on growth.

In short, if trade liberalisation is to be successful in promoting economic development, it needs to avoid adjustment costs as a result of the poor timing and sequencing of liberalisation, and it needs to avoid inegalitarian distributional consequences.

Conclusions

In this chapter we have looked at the theory and measurement of trade liberalisation, and reached the preliminary conclusion that, even in theory, trade liberalisation may not be optimal for developing countries, and that developed countries today preach free trade for poor countries that they never practised themselves in their own pursuit of economic development. There are static gains from trade, according to the law of comparative advantage, assuming continuous full employment. There are also potential dynamic gains from trade, but not if countries get locked into a production and trade structure of goods with low growth potential subject to diminishing returns, which are the attributes of the vast majority of primary commodities. The Heckscher–Ohlin theorem predicts the convergence of factor prices across countries, but there is no evidence for this in the modern world (see Chapter 4).

Despite reservations about the benefits of trade liberalisation for developing countries, the free trade doctrine is presented like a mantra by all the international organisations concerned with economic development, and by major developed countries that dominate the world economy, particularly the United States and the countries of the European Union. The so-called Washington Consensus has become the orthodoxy for countries to follow. World trade only started to be freed in a serious way in developed countries, however, after 1960, while developing countries were given 'policy space' until much later – the early 1980s. Since the debt crisis of that period, the pressure on poor developing countries has been immense to dismantle restrictions on trade, often as part of conditionality and structural adjustment programmes imposed by the IMF and World Bank. The record, however, does not inspire confidence. Many countries in Africa and Latin America have performed much worse in the post-liberalisation era than in the pre-liberalisation era. Most Asian countries have performed well, but they liberalised gradually, encouraging export growth while still retaining controls on imports.

We examined the case for protection and outlined at least four legitimate economic arguments for protection that can be welfare-enhancing, but where the arguments arise as a result of domestic distortions, subsidies rather than tariffs are first-best policies. Subsidies have to be financed, however, either out of general taxation or tariff revenue. There is a case for discrimination against importing goods on the basis of whether they are necessities for consumption and development and whether they are luxury goods. There is a case for high tariffs on the latter both on distributional grounds and to raise revenue. Given the economic arguments for protection, it is not surprising to find, as Chang (2002) documents so convincingly, that the now-developed countries all practised protection in the early stages of their development to foster infant industries. Britain was the first country to go down the free trade route, but only after it had already secured industrial supremacy in the mid-19th century and was able to 'kick away the ladder'. If the United States had taken Adam Smith's anti-protectionist advice, it would still be an economic backwater, yet today it is at the forefront of preaching the free trade gospel to countries at levels of living that the US experienced more than 150 years ago. The historical evidence shows a positive relation between trade restrictions and economic growth.

Finally, we looked at various measures of protection and trade liberalisation, and concluded that the process of liberalisation is a multi-dimensional concept with many facets, and is probably best measured by indices which take a number of variables into account, and not simply by the level of nominal tariffs or the ratio of trade to GDP. Both these obvious measures are fraught with problems in attempting to measure the degree of trade restrictions or trade distortions. What is most important in the trade liberalisation process, if it is to be 'successful', is to get right the timing and sequencing, particularly the relationship between the dismantling of import restrictions and the promotion of exports, otherwise balance of payments difficulties are likely to arise. Exchange rate policy must complement liberalisation and not work against it. Latin America provides a case study in how not to liberalise, while the approach in East Asia of gradual liberalisation, with the focus on export promotion while controlling imports, can be taken as a more exemplary model.

Notes

1. Paul Samuelson (1962) cites it as one of the few laws in economics 'that is both true and non-trivial'.
2. The story is told that when Samuelson visited Cambridge, England with his 1948 paper with him, he showed it to Pigou who asked Samuelson 'have you shown the paper to a mathematician?', to which Samuelson replied 'I am a mathematician', to which Pigou responded 'I mean a British mathematician!'
3. Not compared to the labour intensity of actual imports, the data for which were not available at the time.
4. He later changed his mind about tariffs being the first-best policy and recommended subsidies instead.
5. Rodrik (1992) has argued that even though domestic prices may be higher than world prices with protection, under imperfect competition, marginal costs may be lower. Liberalisation that lowers domestic output will raise cost per unit of output if there are scale economies and technological effort is related to size.

6. See book 4, chapter 2 of the *Wealth of Nations*.
7. It should be noted that Harry Johnson denied the existence of terms of trade deterioration for primary products and for developing countries, and called the terms of trade argument for protection a 'non-argument'.
8. See also Senghaas (1985) for an earlier exploration of how Europe, the US and Scandinavia developed on the basis of protection. Since writing this book, similar evidence has been provided by Reinert (2007).

2. Trade liberalisation, trade performance and economic growth

[T]rade policy provides an enabling environment for development. It does not guarantee the enterprises will take advantage of this environment, nor that private investment will be stimulated. As the recent literature on trade and growth underscores, it certainly does not guarantee adequate levels of economic growth in the long run. Therefore, claims on behalf of liberalisation should be modest lest policy-makers become disillusioned once again. (Rodrik, 1992)

Introduction

In this chapter we shall examine the empirical evidence on the impact of trade liberalisation on export performance, import growth, the balance of payments and then on the economic growth of countries that have liberalised, but first it is important to understand why exports are so crucial for economic development. The first is the neoclassical supply-side argument which focuses on the static and dynamic gains from trade and particularly on the externalities that the export sector can confer on the non-export sector and the rest of the economy. The second is the balance of payments argument that development requires imports that can only be paid for by exports, otherwise growth and development runs up against a balance of payments constraint on demand and growth. The third argument is the virtuous circle model of export-led growth whereby growth caused by exports has positive feedback effects on exports themselves arising from induced productivity growth – summed up by the aphorism 'success breeds success' (but failure breeds failure). Centre–periphery models of growth and development employ the idea of virtuous and vicious circles leading to polarisation in the world economy (see Chapter 3). The first model is the conventional orthodox model which fits nicely into mainstream neoclassical growth theory and its successor, 'new' endogenous growth theory. The other two models – the balance of payments constrained growth model and the export-led growth model – are rarely articulated in the orthodox trade and growth literature, and yet may be of greater importance for understanding growth rate differences in open developing economies, especially if most developing economies are constrained in their performance by a shortage of foreign exchange.

The orthodox neoclassical supply-side model of the relation between exports and growth assumes that the export sector, because of its exposure to foreign competition, confers externalities on the non-export sector, and that the export sector has a higher level of productivity than the non-export sector. Thus, the share of exports in GDP, and the growth of exports, both matter for overall growth performance. Feder (1983) was the first to provide a formal model of this type to explain the relationship between export growth and output growth. 'New' growth theory equations to explain growth rate differences between countries often include the share of trade in GDP as a measure of 'openness' (for example, Knight et al., 1993), but, interestingly, not the *growth* of exports. In the Feder model, the output of the export sector is assumed to be a function of labour and capital in the sector; the output of the non-export sector is assumed to be a function of labour, capital and the output of the export sector (to capture externalities), and the ratio of the respective marginal factor productivities in the two sectors is assumed to deviate from unity by a factor δ. These assumptions produce an augmented neoclassical growth equation of the form:

$$g = a(I/Y) + b(dL/L) + [\delta(1 + \delta)F_x(X/Y)(dX/X)] \qquad (2.1)$$

where I/Y is the investment ratio (as a proxy for the growth of capital), dL/L is the growth of the labour force, dX/X is the growth of exports, X/Y is the share of exports in GDP, $(1 + \delta)$ is the differential productivity effect, and F_x is the externality effect. Feder first tested the model taking a cross-section of 19 semi-industrialised countries and a larger sample of 31 countries over the period 1964–73. The inclusion of dX/X considerably improves the explanatory power of the equation, and the effect of export growth is always statistically significant. The coefficient on export growth in equation (2.1), however, is an amalgam of an externality effect (F_x) and a differential productivity effect (δ). To decompose the two, equation (2.1) can be fitted excluding the export share term (X/Y) which then isolates the externality effect. The difference between the total effect of export growth and the externality effect is the differential productivity effect. When this is done Feder found substantial differences in productivity between the export and non-export sectors, and also evidence of externalities. The results should not surprise us. The export sector is likely to be more 'modern' and capital-intensive than the non-export sector which to a large extent consists of low-productivity agriculture and petty service activities. The externalities conferred by the export sector are part of the dynamic gains from trade associated with the transmission and diffusion of new ideas from abroad relating to both production techniques and more efficient management practices.

The Feder model is a pure supply-side model which has plausibility, but there are other (non-neoclassical) supply-side arguments, as well as demand-side considerations, which would be consistent with finding export growth and GDP growth positively correlated. From the supply side, export growth may raise output growth through externalities, but faster export growth also permits faster import growth. If countries are short of foreign exchange, and domestic and foreign resources are not fully substitutable, more imports permit a fuller use of domestic resources. In particular, more foreign exchange allows the greater import of capital goods which cannot be produced domestically.

This leads on to the role of exports in relaxing a foreign exchange constraint on the demand for output. All components of domestic demand – consumption, investment, government expend- iture and exports themselves – have an import content that needs to be paid for. Exports as a com- ponent of demand are unique in this respect, because exports are the only component of demand that provide the foreign exchange to pay for the imports of other components of demand, which otherwise would be constrained. It is important to stress this, because this insight lies at the heart of demand-oriented theories of growth in an open economy. Most factors in the growth and development process are endogenous to demand, and not exogenously determined as neoclassical growth theory assumes. Capital is a produced means of production and is as much a conse- quence of the growth of output as its cause. The demand for labour is a derived demand from output. Labour input responds to demand in a variety of ways through reductions in unemploy- ment, increases in labour force participation, increases in hours worked, shifts in the labour force from low-productivity to high-productivity sectors, and through international migration. In labour surplus economies, such as developing countries, it stretches credulity to assume an exogenously give supply of labour that determines output in a causal sense. Productivity growth is also largely endogenous to output growth working through induced capital accumulation, embodied technical progress, and static and dynamic returns to scale. To understand growth rate differences between countries, it is necessary to understand why demand growth differs between countries, and the constraints on demand that exist within countries. In most developing countries, the major constraint on the growth of demand is the state of the current account of the balance of payments and the availability of foreign exchange. Export growth relaxes a balance of payments constraint on demand and allows all other components of demand to grow faster without running into balance of payments difficulties. This is the simplest of all explanations of the relationship between exports and output growth.[1]

Finally, fast growth may set off a virtuous circle of growth in which exports and growth interact in a cumulative process with exports driving growth, and fast growth making the export sector more competitive. This raises the question of causality but, more importantly, such 'cumulative' models provide an explanation of why growth and development through trade tends to be concentrated in particular areas of the world, while other regions and countries have been left behind. These models – sometimes also called centre–periphery models – provide a challenge to both orthodox growth theory and trade theory which predict the long-run convergence of living standards across the world. In neoclassical growth theory, capital is assumed to be subject to diminishing returns, so that rich countries, with a lot of capital per head, should grow slower than poor countries, with a smaller amount of capital per head, for the same amount of investment undertaken. Neoclassical trade theory predicts convergence through the assumption of factor price equalisation, as discussed in the previous chapter. Unfortunately, the empirical evidence is at odds with the theory; there is no evidence that living standards across the world are converging, as we shall document in the next chapter.

A simple 'cumulative' model, driven by exports, as the major component of autonomous demand (see Kaldor, 1970; Dixon and Thirlwall, 1975), is to assume that (i) output growth is a function of export growth; (ii) export growth is a function of price competitiveness and foreign income growth; (iii) price competitiveness is a function of wage growth and productivity growth, and (iv) productivity growth is a function of output growth – the so-called Verdoorn Law – working through static and dynamic returns to scale, including learning by doing. It is this induced productivity growth that makes the model 'circular and cumulative' since if fast output growth (caused by export growth) induces faster productivity growth, this makes domestic goods more competitive and therefore induces faster export growth. Suppose, for example, that an economy obtains an advantage in the production of goods with a high income elasticity of demand in world markets, such as high-technology goods, which raises its growth rate above other countries. Through the 'Verdoorn effect', productivity growth will be higher and the economy will retain its competitive advantage in these goods, making it difficult, without protection or exceptional industrial enterprise, for other countries to establish the same commodities. In such a 'cumulative' model, it is the difference between the income elasticity characteristics of exports and imports which is the essence of divergence between industrial and agricultural economies or regions, or between 'centre' and 'periphery'. In fact, it can be shown (Thirlwall, 1979) that if relative prices in international trade are constant and long-run balance of payments equilibrium on current account is a requirement for countries, then one country's growth rate (g) relative to all others (z) is equiproportional to the ratio of the income elasticities of demand for a country's exports (ε) and imports (π), that is:

$$\frac{g}{z} = \frac{\varepsilon}{\pi}, \text{ or } g = \frac{x}{\pi} \qquad (2.2)$$

where εz is the growth of exports (x) and $g\pi$ is the growth of imports (m), both determined by income growth alone. This is the essence of the classic centre–periphery models of Raul Prebisch, Dudley Seers, Nicholas Kaldor and others (see Thirlwall, 1983), and equation (2.2) is sometimes called the

45-degree rule for obvious reasons.[2] Poor developing countries typically export goods with a low income elasticity of demand and import goods with a high income elasticity of demand, compared to developed countries. This simple model can go a long way in explaining differences in the level of development between countries and the forces which perpetuate divergences in the world economy. The forces are *structural* relating to the production and demand characteristics of the goods produced and traded.

In the rest of this chapter we examine the direct impact of trade liberalisation on export growth, import growth and the balance of payments, and then we survey the vast literature first on trade liberalisation, exports and economic performance, and secondly the studies which examine the impact of trade liberalisation on economic growth directly. At the end we shall draw some conclusions.

Trade Liberalisation and Export Growth

There are two broad types of empirical work on the relationship between trade liberalisation and export performance. Firstly, there are large multi-country studies that examine in detail the process of trade policy reforms within individual countries, and its consequences. Pioneer studies of this genre include Little et al. (1970); Balassa (1971); Krueger (1978); Bhagwati (1978), and Michaely et al. (1991). Secondly, there are econometric studies using time-series, cross-section or panel data analysis (pooling time-series and cross-country data). In cross-country analysis some interesting questions arise. Does export performance depend on the liberalisation process itself or mainly on complementary internal reforms and world economic conditions? What are the precise channels through which liberalisation affects export performance? And is there a minimum threshold level of development that a country needs to reach in order for liberalisation to impact significantly on export growth?

Because various forms of trade restrictions, including export duties, cause anti-export bias, the presumption must be that trade liberalisation will raise the growth of exports. But, by how much; and is the quantitative effect enough to offset the growth of imports? These are the pertinent questions. In the countries that have liberalised trade in the last 30 years or so, the main trade reforms to promote exports have included: (i) the reduction or elimination of export duties; (ii) the introduction of tax concessions, including duty drawback schemes allowing firms to reclaim taxes paid on imported inputs used in exports; (iii) tariff reforms to reduce anti-export bias so that it is at least as profitable to produce for export as it is for the home market; (iv) the lifting of administrative barriers to exporting, including export licensing; (v) the liberalisation of regulations governing foreign direct investment; (vi) foreign exchange retention schemes, allowing exporters to retain foreign exchange for the purchase of imported inputs, and (vii) the establishment of export processing zones (see Santos-Paulino, 2002a).

Research on the quantitative relationship between trade liberalisation and export growth gives mixed and conflicting results, which suggest that the context in which trade liberalisation takes place is of primary importance, particularly world economic conditions and domestic economic policies being pursued at the same time. Some studies examine individual countries using time-series analysis; other studies take a cross-section of countries, either treating each country as a single observation, or combining time-series and cross-section observations and applying panel data analysis.

Individual country (or industry) case studies that show a positive effect of liberalisation on export performance include Joshi and Little's (1996) analysis of India's trade reforms in 1991; Ahmed's (2000) study of Bangladesh; the Weiss (1992) and Jenkins (1996) study of manufactured exports from Mexico and Bolivia, and Pacheco-López's (2005) study of Mexico after the trade reforms of 1985/86.[3] Multi-country case studies that show a positive impact of liberalisation on export growth include Thomas's et al. (1991) cross-section analysis; Helleiner's (1994) collection of theoretical and empirical studies; and Bleaney's (1999) panel data study of manufactured exports for ten countries of Latin America.

Other studies, however, have found little or no significant relationship between trade liberalisation and export growth. These include UNCTAD's (1989) analysis of trade reforms and export performance in the least developed countries; other studies under the auspices of UNCTAD by Agosin (1991) and Shafaeddin (1994); Clarke and Kirkpatrick's (1992) cross-section analysis, and the time-series work of Greenaway and Sapsford (1994) and Greenaway, Leybourne and Sapsford (1997).

Part of the reasons for the differences in the results obtained is not only context, but also differences in how liberalisation is measured and the methodology used, particularly in the econometric studies. The most comprehensive recent study is that by Santos-Paulino and Thirlwall (2004) (see also Santos-Paulino, 2002a) who take a panel of 22 developing countries from the four 'regions' of Africa, Latin America, East Asia and South Asia that undertook significant trade liberalisation during the period 1972–97. Trade liberalisation is measured by two indicators: firstly by the ratio of export duties to export revenue (as a measure of the tax on exports), and secondly by a dummy variable which takes the value of one in the year when significant trade liberalisation took place (and continued) and zero otherwise. Panel data and time-series/cross-section estimation techniques are then applied to the determination of export growth using a conventional export growth equation of the form:

$$x_t = a_0 + a_1(rer_t) + a_2(z_t) + a_3(d_{xt}) + a_4(lib_t) \quad (2.3)$$

where x is the growth of export volume; a_0 is a constant; rer is the rate of change of the real exchange rate; z is the growth of world income; d_x is the export duty variable, lib is the liberalisation dummy, and t is a time subscript.

Depending on the estimation technique used,[4] the central estimate is that trade liberalisation has raised export growth by approximately two percentage points, or by approximately 25 per cent compared with the pre-liberalisation export growth rate. The estimated coefficient on the export duty variable (d) is negative and statistically significant, but the coefficient is small (roughly -0.2). The estimated coefficient on the liberalisation dummy variable (lib) is consistently in the range 1–2 taking the full sample of 22 countries, but the quantitative effect (shown in brackets) differs between the four regions: Africa (3.58), South Asia (2.54), East Asia (2.42) and Latin America (1.66). For a country's overall economic performance to improve, however, it is not enough for export growth to accelerate. Export growth must be shown to outpace import growth, otherwise balance of payments difficulties will arise.

Trade Liberalisation and Import Growth

Most of the orthodox literature on trade liberalisation and trade performance has focused on exports. Very little attention has been paid to import growth, or the balance between export and import growth. This is a serious weakness of trade liberalisation studies, but is a reflection of the fact that in orthodox trade and growth theory, the balance of payments is either assumed to look after itself, or deficits are regarded as a form of consumption smoothing and have no long-run effect on real variables. The main function of tariffs and non-tariff barriers, such as quantitative import controls, quality standards and government procurement policies, is to control the level and growth of imports in order to protect and promote domestic industry. If tariffs are reduced, and quantitative restrictions are lifted, imports can be expected to increase. There will be an 'autonomous' increase, and in addition imports are likely to become more sensitive to income and relative price changes domestically. If the income elasticity of demand for imports increases, this tightens a balance of payments constraint on growth (see later). Country studies by Melo and Vogt (1984) for Venezuela; Mah (1999) for Thailand, and Bertola and Faini (1991) for Morocco all show a significant impact of trade liberalisation on the growth of imports and the sensitivity of imports to domestic income growth. The most comprehensive study to date, however, of the relationship between trade liberalisation and import growth is that by Santos-Paulino and Thirlwall (2004) (see also Santos-Paulino, 2002b) who take the same 22 countries as for export growth, discussed previously, and test four hypotheses: firstly, that the switch from a protective to a more liberal trading system will have a direct and continuing impact on import growth from the time of liberalisation, which can be captured by a shift dummy variable in an equation to explain import growth (as equation (2.3) for export growth); secondly, that tariff reductions raise import growth; thirdly, that a more liberal trade regime increases the income (and price) elasticity of demand for imports, and finally, the impact of liberalisation is greater the higher the initial degree of protection. The import growth equation specified to capture these effects is:

$$m_t = b_0 + b_1(rer_t) + b_2(y_t) + b_3(d_{mt}) + b_4(lib_t) \\ + b_5(liby_t) + b_6(librer_t) \qquad (2.4)$$

where m is the growth of imports, b_0 is a constant; rer is the rate of change of the real exchange rate; y is the growth of domestic income; d_m is the average tariff rate on imports; lib is a shift dummy variable which takes the value of 1 from the year of significant liberalisation, and zero otherwise, and $liby$ and $librer$ are interaction terms between liberalisation and income growth and the real exchange rate, respectively, to test whether liberalisation increases the income and price elasticities of demand for imports. The equation was fitted to the panel of 22 developing countries discussed earlier, using the same econometric methodology as for the analysis of export growth, and disaggregating the sample according to the initial level of protection: low, moderate, high or very high (as measured by the Heritage Foundation Trade Policy Grading Scale). The results may be summarised as follows. Trade liberalisation itself, controlling for all other factors, has increased the growth of imports by between 5 and 6 percentage points (although by less in countries with already a low or moderate degree of protection). The independent effect of tariff cuts has been to raise the growth of imports by between 0.2 and 0.5 percentage points for a one percentage point cut in the tariff rate. Liberalisation has increased the elasticity of imports to domestic income and exchange rate changes by a small amount of between 0.2 and 0.5 percentage points.

Overall, it seems that liberalisation across the whole sample of countries increased import growth by about 6 percentage points, which represents a near doubling of the pre-liberalisation import growth. This compares with the increase in the export growth rate for the same sample of countries of 2 percentage points, or a 25 per cent increase compared to the pre-liberalisation period.

We have examined ourselves (Pacheco-López and Thirlwall, 2006) the direct effect of trade liberalisation on the income elasticity of demand for imports for 17 Latin American countries over the period 1977–2002, using a simplified version of equation (2.4):

$$m_t = c_0 + c_1(rer_t) + \pi_1(y_t) + \pi_2(liby_t) \qquad (2.5)$$

where π_1 is the income elasticity of demand for imports in the pre-liberalisation period and $(\pi_1 + \pi_2)$ is the income elasticity of demand for imports in the post-liberalisation period. Fitting a pooled time-series/cross-section estimator (with 425 observations) to the data gives:

$$m_t = -0.74 - 0.066(rer_t) + 2.08(y_t) + 0.55(liby_t) \quad (2.6)$$
$$\quad (-2.21) \quad (-5.56) \qquad (25.07) \qquad (4.44)$$

where the bracketed terms are t-ratios. The income elasticity of demand for imports is estimated at 2.08 in the pre-liberalisation period, and it increases by 0.55 (to 2.63) in the post-liberalisation period. This increase more or less offsets the increase in export growth post-liberalisation, leaving the GDP growth rate of countries consistent with balance of payments equilibrium virtually unchanged. If we use the simple balance of payments-constrained growth formula of $g = x/\pi$ (see equation (2.2)), we get a predicted growth rate for the Latin American countries pre-liberalisation of: $g = 4.61$ per cent/$2.08 = 2.22$ per cent compared to the actual growth rate of 2.02 per cent; and for the post-liberalisation period we get: $g = 5.93$ per cent/$2.63 = 2.25$ per cent, compared to the actual growth rate of 3.23 per cent. The faster actual growth rate post-liberalisation is reflected in a deterioration in the current account of the balance of payments financed by capital inflows.

This increase in the income elasticity of demand for imports in Latin America as a result of trade liberalisation is confirmed using the technique of rolling regressions taking 13 overlapping periods starting from 1977–90 and ending in 1989–2002. The estimated income elasticity starts at 2.04

and ends at 2.82, giving an annual trend rate of increase of approximately 0.04 percentage points. Applying the same technique to the 17 countries individually gives mixed results. In Argentina, Brazil and Peru there is a steady increase in the elasticity through time. In Bolivia, the Dominican Republic, Guatemala and Paraguay there is a sudden jump in the mid-1980s. On the other hand, in Honduras, Nicaragua and Venezuela there seems to have been a decrease in the elasticity, while in Uruguay and Costa Rica, the elasticity seems to have been relatively constant.

Trade Liberalisation and the Balance of Payments

If trade liberalisation raises the growth of imports by more than exports, or raises the income elasticity of demand for imports by more than in proportion to the growth of exports, the balance of payments of trade (or payments) will worsen for a given growth of output, unless the currency can be manipulated to raise the value of exports relative to output. Surprisingly, very little research has been done on the balance of payments effects of trade liberalisation, but even advocates of trade liberalisation for developing countries recognise deterioration as a distinct possibility. Dornbusch (1992), for example, writes:

> because of balance of payments problems, comprehensive trade reform requires one of two conditions: either the country must be politically in a position to have a major

real depreciation of the exchange rate (to help boost exports) or else it must have access to foreign exchange for a substantial period of time . . . If reserves are not available and depreciation is impractical, the only realistic option for trade policy is to approach liberalisation more gradually. (p. 82)

Krueger (1978), one of the most ardent advocates of trade liberalisation, admits to the possibility of 'temporary' balance of payments problems. One of the early studies on this topic by Khan and Zahler (1985) examined the effects of trade and financial liberalisation on the economies of Argentina, Chile and Uruguay and found that the current account went into severe deficit, and that capital flows generated by interest rate differentials were not sufficient to finance the deficits without severe income contraction as well. Vos et al. (2002) remark in their survey of liberalisation in a selection of Latin American and Caribbean countries that: 'higher import demand and typically lagging exports meant that the trade deficit went up for a given level of output' and 'higher import propensities offset the growth impacts of export expansion that nearly all countries witnessed. Although exports gained importance as a source of growth . . . the gains do not seem to have been so strong as originally supposed by advocates of liberalisation'.

The first rigorous econometric study of the impact of trade liberalisation on the trade balance of developing countries was by Parikh for UNCTAD (1999) who took 16 countries over the period 1970–95, and fitted the following equation using panel data techniques:

$$\frac{TB_t}{GDP_t} = a_1 + b_1(y_t) + c_1(z_t) + d_1(tt_t) + e_1(lib_t) \quad (2.7)$$

where *TB* is the trade balance (deflated by GDP to allow for differences in the size of countries); *y* is the growth of domestic income; *z* is the growth of world income; *tt* is the terms of trade, and *lib* is a dummy variable using the Sachs and Warner (1995) openness index. The main result is that trade liberalisation (or openness) seems to have worsened the trade balance by 2.7 per cent of GDP, which is substantial. In later work for WIDER, Parikh (2002) extends the analysis to 64 countries and obtains weaker results for the direct effect of liberalisation on the trade balance, but finds a strong negative effect through terms of trade deterioration after liberalisation has taken place. On the other hand, looking in detail at the import and export performance of 15 countries before and after liberalisation, he finds that in 11 countries imports grew faster than exports, and concludes:

> the exports of most of the liberalising countries have not grown fast enough after trade liberalisation to compensate for the rapid growth of imports during the years immediately following trade liberalisation. The evidence suggests that trade liberalisation in developing countries has tended to lead to a deterioration in the trade account. (pp. 16–17)

Santos-Paulino and Thirlwall (2004) (see also Santos-Paulino, 2004) take the same basic model as Parikh, but extend it to include other control variables, and also examine the current account of the balance of payments as well as the trade balance. They take the same sample of 22 developing countries as for the impact of trade liberalisation on export and import growth previously discussed, and specify the following equation:

$$\frac{TB_t}{GDP_t} \text{and} \frac{BP_t}{GDP_t} = d_0 + d_1(z) + d_2(y_t) + d_3(rer_t) +$$
$$d_4(d_{xt}) + d_5(d_{mt}) + d_6(tt_t) +$$
$$d_7(lib_t) + d_8(liby_t) \qquad (2.8)$$

where TB and BP are the trade balance and current account balance of payments, respectively (normalised by GDP); z is world income growth; y is domestic income growth; rer is the rate of change of the real exchange rate; d_x is the average duty on exports; d_m is the average duty on imports; lib is a shift dummy variable for the year of trade liberalisation; $liby$ is an interaction term which measures the change in the sensitivity of the balance of trade or payments to income growth following liberalisation; tt is the ratio of export prices to import prices (or terms of trade) and is included in the equation because the trade balance and current account are measured in monetary terms. The equations are estimated using panel data techniques over the period 1976–98, and yield some interesting results. In the case of the trade balance it is found that world income growth of 1 per cent leads to an improvement equal to 0.7 per cent of

GDP; domestic income growth of 1 per cent reduces the trade balance by 0.2 per cent of GDP; the real exchange rate has hardly any effect on the trade balance, nor do terms of trade changes; a 1 per cent reduction in export duties improves the trade balance by 0.2 per cent of GDP, while a reduction in import tariffs by 1 per cent worsens the trade balance by the same amount; and liberalisation has increased the coefficient of the trade balance ratio to domestic income changes by about −0.3. Most important for our purposes here, the switch to a more liberal trading regime has worsened, on average, the trade balance by approximately 2 per cent of GDP, which is similar to the estimate by Parikh in UNCTAD (1999).

In the case of the current account/GDP ratio, however, the impact of trade liberalisation is estimated to be slightly less; a worsening of between 0.5 and 1.0 per cent of GDP. The explanation for the difference is either favourable movements on the invisible account (or non-merchandise trade account) of the balance of payments, or that countries were not able to sustain current deficits equal to the deterioration in the trade balance and had to deflate their economies accordingly. Santos-Paulino (2007) finds similar results for a group of 17 Least Developed Countries[5] over the period 1970–2001. Trade liberalisation raised export growth by about 0.5 percentage points, but import growth by over one percentage point, leading to a deterioration in the trade balance of 4 per cent of GDP. The deterioration in the current account, however, was less.

In our own research (Pacheco-López and Thirlwall, 2007) we have focused on the balance of trade effects of trade liberalisation in 17 Latin American countries over the period 1977–2002. Using either a panel data estimator (with random or fixed effects) or a time-series/cross-section estimator, and controlling for world income growth, domestic income growth and changes in the real exchange rate, we estimate a deterioration in the trade balance of between 1.3 and 2.3 per cent of GDP.

All these results show that trade liberalisation has not, in general, improved the trade-off between GDP growth and the balance of trade (or payments); on the contrary, the trade-off has deteriorated, making sustainable growth more difficult (see later). Reisen's (1998) work on trade deficits in Latin America and Asia suggests a range of sustainable deficits of between 1.6 and 3.8 per cent of GDP, providing the existing level of international debt relative to GDP is not more than 50 per cent, and the level of foreign currency reserves covers at least six months of imports. Many developing countries, however, have ratios of debt to GDP far in excess of 50 per cent, and reserves much lower than necessary to pay for six months of imports, which means that sustainable deficits are probably not more than 1–2 per cent of GDP in the long run (unless financed by pure aid). Any increase in the trade or current account deficit more than this, resulting from the trade liberalisation process, is therefore either likely to trigger a currency crisis or necessitate a severe deflation of domestic demand. As UNCTAD (2004) argues in its *Least Developed Countries Report 2004* on the theme of linking international trade with poverty reduction: 'this critical [balance of payments] constraint on development and sustained poverty reduction is conspicuously absent in the current debate on trade and poverty'; and we might add, in parenthesis, also in the debate on trade liberalisation. The balance of payments consequences are generally ignored, consistent with orthodox theory.

Trade Liberalisation and Economic Performance

We now come to the crucial question of whether there is conclusive evidence that trade liberalisation has significantly improved the overall economic performance of countries in the sense of raising the rate of growth of GDP or GDP per capita, leading to a substantial rise in the average standard of living. The analysis up to now would suggest that the impact may be weak. On the one hand, it seems fairly clear that trade liberalisation has benefited exporters, but on the other hand there has been increased import penetration as a result of the reduction in tariffs and non-tariff barriers to trade, and a deterioration of the balance of trade and payments in most countries, which may have constrained growth.

There are several analytical difficulties in conducting research in this area, and in assessing the results. The first is knowing the counterfactual, that is what would have happened in the absence of trade liberalisation? To answer this question, some researchers do 'before and after' studies comparing economic performance some years before and some years after, and others try to compare liberalising countries with a control group that have not liberalised, but in neither of these approaches is it easy to control for other factors that may be affecting economic performance either before or after liberalisation or between countries. Indeed, a major problem in interpreting the data is that trade liberalisation tends to go hand in hand with domestic economic reforms, so that studies of liberalisation and economic performance may be biased to the extent that the measures of trade liberalisation or openness that are used are collinear with domestic policies, particularly if trade liberalisation has been initiated as part of structural adjustment programmes which may impact favourably or adversely on growth performance. The only way to cope satisfactorily with the question of the counterfactual, and to control for the effect of other variables on economic performance, is to do rigorous econometric analysis using the dummy variable technique to distinguish between pre-liberalisation and post-liberalisation periods and/or between liberalised and non-liberalised economies, using cross-section data, time-series data for individual countries, or panel data analysis (combining cross-section and times-series observations). This is the approach generally taken by researchers, but what we shall find is that the results are often sensitive to the measure of liberalisation taken, the time period of analysis, the sample of countries, and whether cross-section, time-series or panel data analysis is used. In this sense, the jury is still out on the question of whether trade liberalisation is good for growth. It may be or may not depending on the circumstances of the country concerned. What we can say is that the extravagant promises of the pro-trade liberalisers look hollow when compared to the evidence.

Nonetheless, let us now consider some of the major results in the field, and then try and reach some conclusions at the end. We shall see that some studies do show a favourable impact of liberalisation on economic performance, but the studies have their critics, while other studies are ambiguous or inconclusive. One of the earliest major studies of trade orientation, trade distortions and growth in developing countries was by Sebastian Edwards (1992), who develops a model which assumes that more open economies are more efficient at absorbing exogenously generated technology. Using various indicators of trade distortions constructed by Leamer (1988), he shows for a sample of 30 developing countries over the period 1970–82 that more open economies tend to grow faster. To test the hypothesis, a conventional growth equation is used relating the growth of per capita income of countries to their investment ratio; to their initial level of per capita income as a proxy for technological backwardness, and to the various measures of trade distortion. All but one of the trade distortion measures produce a significant negative coefficient, and the findings are apparently robust with respect to the sample taken, the time period taken, and the method of estimation. The findings also appear robust with respect to alternative indicators of trade liberalisation and openness such as the average import tariff; an index of the effective rate of protection; the average black market exchange rate premium, and the World Bank's (1987) index of outward orientation. In a similar study for 93 developed and developing countries over the period 1960–90, Edwards (1998) regresses total factor productivity growth on nine indicators of openness listed earlier on pages 53–54, and six turn out to be significant with the expected sign, using the initial level of per capita income and differences in education as control variables. Edwards concludes 'these results are quite remarkable, suggesting with tremendous consistency that there is a significantly positive relationship between openness and productivity growth'. Rodriguez and Rodrik (2000), however, have criticised the estimation method used of weighted least squares where the weighting variable is a country's per capita income, giving a weight to the US 100 times that of the poorest country in the sample. Using more reasonable weights (with variables measured in logarithms), Edwards's results lose much of their significance. Of the 19 different equations reported, only three are now statistically significant. Rodriguez and Rodrik conclude 'we do not concur with Edwards's assertion that the cross-country data reveal the existence of a robust relationship between openness and productivity or GDP growth'. They themselves can find no statistically significant relationship between either import duties or the percentage of imports covered by non-tariff barriers and the growth of per capita income over the period 1975–94, controlling for the initial level of per capita income and education.

In another comprehensive study, Dollar (1992) also addresses the question of whether outward-oriented developing countries grow more rapidly, taking a sample of 95 countries over the period 1976–85, but using different measures of trade orientation to those used by Edwards. Two measures of distortion are used: first an index of real exchange rate distortion, and second an index of real exchange rate variability. The presumption is that a high *relative* price level in a country over many years is indicative of strong protection and incentives geared to production for the home market. Growth equations are first estimated across countries using each country's measure of exchange rate distortion, controlling for differences in the level of investment and exchange rate variability. Dollar finds that, on average, trade distortions in Africa and Latin America reduced the growth of income per head by between 1.5 and 2.1 per cent per annum. Rodriguez and Rodrik (2000) argue, however, that Dollar's measure of trade distortion is flawed on three counts. Firstly, only tariffs will keep relative prices high. Export duties reduce the domestic price of tradeables relative to the world prices and therefore would lower the measure of distortion. Conversely, and paradoxically, export subsidies would make a country look more protected. Secondly, the measure assumes purchasing power parity (PPP), and that the law of one price holds, so that any deviation of a country's prices from world prices is caused only by trade restrictions. Thirdly, the distortion measure assumes no systematic difference in national price levels due to transport costs. Rodriguez and Rodrik show that over one-half of the variance in Dollar's distortion index is accounted for by geographic factors, and that PPP does not hold. Also, none of Dollar's regressions control for differences in the initial level of per capita income, or for education. When these variables are included, together with dummy variables for different regions of the world, the distortion index is not robust. The variability of the exchange rate, which is a robust variable, is more a measure of macroeconomic instability than trade distortion.

Dollar and Kraay (2004) take a sample of 73 developing countries from the 1970s to the 1990s and rank them according to the increase in their share of trade (exports plus imports) in GDP. The top one-third of countries are called 'the post-1980 globalisers' and these countries (24 in all) are compared with the rest of the sample. Per capita income in the 'globaliser' countries is shown to have grown much more rapidly decade by decade compared to the 'non-globalisers'. In the 'globaliser' countries, where the share of trade more than doubled from 16 per cent to 33 per cent of GDP, the population-weighted growth of per capita income rose from 2.9 per cent per annum in the 1970s, to 3.5 per cent in the 1980s and to 5 per cent in the 1990s. In the other countries, where the share of trade fell from 60 per cent to 49 per cent, per capita income growth fell from 3.3 per cent per annum in the 1970s to 0.8 per cent in the 1980s and to 1.4 per cent in the 1990s. These non-parametric results look convincing on the surface, and have been highly influential in policy circles in the debate on the benefits of trade liberalisation, but unfortunately they are open to a number of criticisms. Firstly, the differential growth rates reported for the two sets of countries are population weighted, and include India and China in the sample of 'globalisers'. If unweighted figures are taken, the record of the 'globalisers' looks much closer to the 'non-globalisers': 3.1 per cent growth in the 1970s, 0.5 per cent in the 1980s and 2.0 per cent in the 1990s. Second, Dowrick and Golley (2004) show that the more favourable performance of the 'globalisers' is entirely due to the rapid growth of India and China, particularly in the 1990s. If India and China are excluded from the sample, the remaining 22 'globalised' countries grew slower over the period 1980–2000 than the 'non-globalisers', whether or not growth rates are population weighted. Thirdly, and most telling, globalising countries were not the most open or the most liberal. Their share of trade as a percentage of GDP rose the most, but the countries started from a low base and were still less open economies than the 'non-globalisers', at least until the 1990s. Similarly, those countries labelled as 'globalisers' according to the size of their tariff reductions remained continually more closed than the 'non-globalisers' measured by trade volume. Even in the 1990s, the 'non-globalisers' had a trade volume 48 per cent higher as a percentage of GDP than the 'globalisers'. In fact, there turns out to be a very weak link between tariff changes and trade volume. Only 9 of the 73 countries taken experienced both the highest increase in trade shares and the biggest tariff cuts. In the 1990s the tariffs of the 'globalisers' were still higher than the 'non-globalisers'. In short, the non-parametric results of globalisation that Dollar and Kraay present are highly misleading. Their globalising countries did not grow faster, taking India and China out of the sample, nor were they more open or liberal.

However, Dollar and Kraay also perform more rigorous econometric tests of the relation between trade openness and economic growth which are more valuable, but much less euphoric. They take approximately 100 countries during the 1980s and 1990s, and instead of using cross-country differences in trade and growth they use *within-country* variation in the data by taking decadal changes in growth and the volume of trade, which they argue are a good measure of *changes* in trade policy.

Taking decadal changes in the variables also has the advantage of eliminating the effect of geography on trade, or any variable for that matter that does not vary with time. What they find is that, controlling for other variables that may affect changes in growth, the effect of trade openness is positive and significant, but the magnitude of the effect (which they do not comment on) is extremely small. To raise the growth of per capita income by 0.5 to 1.0 percentage points would require an increase in the ratio of trade to GDP of 20 percentage points.

The influence of Dollar and Kraay on the views of the World Bank can be vividly seen in its 2002 report on *Globalisation, Growth and Poverty* in which it claims:

> some 24 developing countries – with 3 billion people – have doubled their ratio of trade to income over the past two decades. The rest of the developing world actually trades less today than it did 20 years ago. The more globalised developing countries have increased their per capita growth rate from 1 per cent in the 1960s to 3 per cent in the 1970s, 4 per cent in the 1980s and 5 per cent in the 1990s. . . . much of the rest of the developing world – with about 2 billion people – is becoming marginalised. Their aggregate growth rate was actually negative in the 1990s. (p. 5)

As we have seen above, however, the World Bank is disingenuous and does not tell the full story.

Another major influential study of trade orientation and growth is that by Sachs and Warner (1995), taking 79 countries over the period 1979–89. They apply the dummy variable technique of giving a country a zero value if its economy is closed and a value of 1 if it is open, using the five criteria mentioned earlier in Chapter 1. It is found that open economies grew on average by 2.44 percentage points faster than closed economies. Rodriguez and Rodrik (2000) argue, however, that it is not tariffs and non-tariff barriers that distinguish the two sets of countries but a combination of the black market exchange rate premium and the State monopoly of exports. The former is highly correlated with turbulent macroeconomic conditions and the latter with location in Africa (the slowest growing continent). All the countries with a black market premium in excess of 20 per cent had serious problems of either debt, terms of trade deterioration or war.

The Sachs–Warner (S–W) index is a composite index of five variables, and clearly captures many other aspects of openness than pure trade policy. Harrison and Hanson (1999) run cross-country growth regressions on each of the five components of the S–W index separately over the period 1970–89, and find that their measures of tariffs and quotas are not significantly related to growth performance. When all five variables comprising the index are included separately in the same regressions, only the dummy variable representing a socialist country is statistically significant.

Wacziarg and Welch (2005) extend the Sachs–Warner analysis into the 1990s when 78 countries are classified as open and 27 closed (compared to 31 open and 74 closed during the period studied by Sachs and Warner). When the S–W regressions are re-run, the 'openness' dummy variable loses its statistical significance; there appears to be no effect of openness on growth. This is also what Kneller (2007) finds using the S–W index taking 37 countries that liberalised and 35 which did not over the period 1970–98 (taking five-year averages of the data). Running regressions only for countries that liberalised show a growth impact of 0.81 percentage points in the five-year period of liberalisation and 2.02 percentage points after liberalisation. When, however, countries that did not liberalise are added to the sample, the results show no significant difference in the growth acceleration of countries. The explanation must be either common shocks to all countries, or that liberalisation made no difference.

Wacziarg and Welch prefer, however, to measure the impact of trade liberalisation using the date of liberalisation as the dummy variable, rather than the dichotomous open/closed S–W dummy. Using panel data to look at the mean difference between liberalised and non-liberalised countries, they find an effect of liberalisation on growth of between 0.5 and 1.5 percentage points, depending on the method of estimation, but there is considerable country heterogeneity. Taking 24 emerging market economies, and comparing per capita income growth three years before and three years after liberalisation, they find a positive effect in 13 countries, and a zero or negative effect in the other 11. One of the major conclusions of the study is that the main channel linking trade and growth is investment. This was the conclusion of an earlier study by Wacziarg (2001) who specifies and examines six channels through which trade openness might effect growth: government economic policy, the size of government, better allocation of resources, capital accumulation, knowledge spillovers and foreign direct investment. Using his own measure of openness based on a weighted average of several indicators, such as tariff revenues, non-tariff barriers and an indicator of outward orientation, the model is applied to 57 countries over the pooled time-periods 1970–74, 1975–79, 1980–84 and 1985–89. It is found that 60 per cent of the total effect of trade policy on growth comes from investment, 22 per cent from technology transfer (proxied by the ratio of manufactured exports to total merchandise exports) and 18 per cent from government macroeconomic policy. Levine and Renelt (1992), in their study of the robustness of variables used in 'new' growth theory, also find a stronger relationship between trade openness and investment than between trade openness and growth.

Greenaway, Morgan and Wright (1998, 2002) examine the relationship between trade liberalisation and growth within a 'new' growth theory framework using panel data analysis for up to 73 countries over the period 1975–93. Different measures of liberalisation are used including the S–W index, an index used by Dean et al. (1994) on the timing of liberalisation, and a dummy variable for the timing of World Bank Structural Adjustment Programmes that contain a requirement of trade reform. Their novel approach, not used by other studies, is to use the liberalisation indices as one-off (impulse) shift dummies with lags, allowing liberalisation time to work. In all cases, they find that the impact of liberalisation in the first year is negative (but not significantly so); in the second year the impact is positive, but not significant, and in the third year it is positive and significant using both the S–W and Dean indices with an impact on growth of between 1.5 and 1.8 per cent. This suggests a J-curve type effect of liberalisation on growth, with the effects taking time to come through. On the other hand, there is no indication of whether the positive impact lasts.

The dummies used to signify World Bank Structural Adjustment Programmes are not significant, probably because the start of these programmes is an ex-ante measure of intent, not a measure of what actually happened. Clarke and Kirkpatrick (1992), however, take 80 countries over the period 1981–88, when Structural Adjustment Programmes were in operation, and find no statistically significant relationship between any of the performance variables they examine (such as GDP growth or export growth) and dummy variables representing trade reform programmes, even taking lags. The authors conclude: 'the overall conclusion of this study must be that there is no empirical evidence to suggest that economic performance benefits from trade reform strategies. This is consistent with the rather ambiguous evidence from other sources'.

An interesting study by Yanikkaya (2003) also highlights the sensitivity of results to the measures of openness and trade restrictions. He takes a panel of over 100 countries (developed and developing) over the period 1970–97 using two broad measures of openness: (i) trade volume measured by the share of exports and imports in GDP, and (ii) trade restrictions of various types. What is found is that trade volume and growth are positively related, so too are levels of trade restrictions and growth, and this latter result is driven by the developing countries in the sample, which is consistent with the predictions of the theoretical literature which we discussed in Chapter 1 that, under certain conditions, developing countries can benefit from trade restrictions. The coefficient on the trade volume variable is + 0.18, the coefficient on the tariff variable is + 0.07 and export taxes also show a positive effect on growth with a coefficient of + 0.05. Yanikkaya concludes 'these results . . . provide support for the infant industry case for protection and for strategic trade policies'. Interestingly, while the East Asian countries are more open than Latin America with regard to trade volume, their average tariff rates are higher. This reflects the difference between the export promotion policies pursued by East Asia and the pure import substitution policies pursued by Latin America.

Dowrick (1997), in his study of 74 countries over the period 1960–90, only finds a positive relationship between trade volume (or the trade intensity ratio) and the growth of per capita income when the population size of countries is controlled for (because a small country naturally trades more since it tends to be more specialised and less able to meet all its own needs). A country's openness is measured as the deviation of its actual trade ratio from that predicted by population size, and the sample is then divided into countries with above and below average openness. On average, the more open economies appear to grow faster at a rate of 3.1 per cent per annum, compared to 2.0 per cent per annum for the more 'closed' economies, but the relation is not linear. A strong relationship is only apparent taking the extremes of the distribution. In the middle of the distribution, the 'closed' countries actually grew faster than the open economies, at 2.4 per cent per annum compared to 2.2 per cent per annum.

The sensitivity of the results to the measures of trade liberalisation used, the time period taken and the method of estimation applied, is also highlighted in a major overview by Harrison (1996). She takes seven different measures of openness and finds that when cross-section data are employed only one of the seven openness measures (the black market exchange rate premium) affects growth significantly, but six of the seven measures are statistically significant using annual (panel) data. The issue of causality is also raised. It is found that where more open trade policies do seem to be associated with higher growth rates, it is also the case that higher growth rates lead to more open trade regimes.

In support of the optimistic camp of trade liberalisation, we see that there is some evidence that trade liberalisation promotes economic growth and a higher rate of growth of living standards; on the other hand, the results are not always robust, and can be criticised from a number of angles. Rodriguez and Rodrik (2000) conclude their evaluation of studies of trade orientation and economic performance by saying that indicators of openness used are either poor measures of trade barriers or are highly correlated with other sources of economic performance. This is not to say that trade protection is good for growth, but it might be so in certain circumstances if protection is able to increase the share of manufacturing output in total GDP which confers growth effects working through externalities and dynamic returns to scale. Rodriguez and Rodrik's concern is that the priority given to trade policy reform has generated expectations that are unlikely to be met, and may crowd out other institutional reforms which would have a greater impact. Trade liberalisation, in other words, cannot be regarded as a panacea, or a substitute for a comprehensive trade and development strategy.

Trade Liberalisation and the Trade-Off Between Growth and the Balance of Payments

The ultimate test of successful trade liberalisation, at least at the macro level, is whether it lifts a

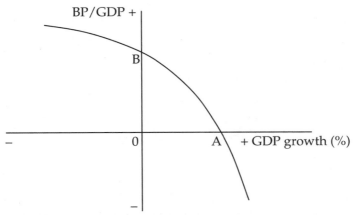

Figure 2.1   *The trade-off between growth and the*
balance of payments

country on to a higher growth path consistent with
a sustainable balance of payments; in other words,
if it improves the trade-off between growth and
the balance of payments. There is always a (negative) trade-off between growth and the balance of
payments, because as growth expands it sucks in
more imports to meet increases in final and intermediate demand, and the balance of payments
worsens. The trade-off is depicted in Figure 2.1

The ratio of the balance of payments to GDP is
measured on the vertical axis and the growth of
GDP (y) on the horizontal axis. The trade-off curve
is drawn non-linear because at higher and higher
growth rates imports are likely to be more and
more sensitive to demand, and the balance of payments deteriorates more quickly. The position of
the trade-off curve indicates the health of the
economy. The further it is to the right, the healthier

it is, because the higher is the growth rate consistent with balance of payment equilibrium. An economy would be in serious trouble if the curve cuts the axes below the origin, showing negative growth and a payments deficit.

One of the ways of testing whether liberalisation has been successful, therefore, is to see whether it has shifted the trade-off curve upwards. We do this (Pacheco-López and Thirlwall, 2007) for 17 Latin American countries over the period 1977–2002 taking the trade balance/GDP ratio as the dependent variable. The technique is first to use empirical data to estimate the trade-off curve, using regression analysis, and then to include a shift dummy in the regression for the year in which each country undertook trade liberalisation in a significant way to estimate whether a significant improvement (or deterioration) in the trade-off can be found. Using pooled data for the 17 Latin American countries over the period 1977–2002 (giving 425 observations), and fitting (for simplicity) a linear regression line, gives the estimated trade-off curve (with t statistics in brackets) of:

$$TB/GDP = -3.203 - 0.315\,y \qquad (2.9)$$
$$(6.3) \qquad (3.3)$$

The slope coefficient is statistically significant with the expected negative sign, and indicates that, on average, a one percentage point change in the growth rate in Latin America as a whole has been associated with an opposite change in the trade balance ratio of 0.315 percentage points. The average growth of GDP for the sample as a whole is 2.76 per cent per annum with a trade deficit of −4.69 per cent of GDP. This is not a particularly healthy situation, but is there any evidence that trade liberalisation has improved it? When a liberalisation dummy (*lib*) for each country is added to the equation the following result is obtained:

$$TB/GDP = -1.387 - 0.258\, y - 3.610\, (lib) \qquad (2.10)$$
$$(2.1) \quad\;\; (2.7) \qquad\;\; (4.2)$$

The slope coefficient falls slightly compared to equation (2.9), but the significant finding is that the coefficient on the liberalisation dummy is *negative*, not positive. In other words, trade liberalisation in Latin America has, on average, *worsened* the trade-off between growth and the trade balance, not improved it. The result is confirmed using more sophisticated econometric techniques in a full model of trade balance determination which also controls for other variables such as changes in the real exchange rate and world income growth. The estimated coefficient on the liberalisation dummy falls from −3.6 to −2.0, but is still significantly negative. Applying the same methodology to each individual country shows the impact of trade liberalisation to be positive in only two countries: Chile and Venezuela. In Chile the trade-off improved because of the more gradual approach to liberalisation, and more attention paid to sequencing. In Venezuela, the improvement in the trade-off coincides with the huge benefits from oil. The technique of estimating the trade-off between growth and the balance of trade (payments), and determining whether trade liberalisation has improved the trade-off significantly, could be more widely applied to other continents and countries.

Conclusions

The overall conclusion of this chapter is that research on the impact of trade liberalisation on the trade performance and the growth of living standards in developing countries gives mixed results. They seem to depend on the sample of countries taken, the time period of analysis; the measure of trade liberalisation used; what variables are controlled for, and the statistical method(s) of estimation. Nonetheless, some broad conclusions can be reached. Trade liberalisation has improved the export performance of countries (by as much as 2 percentage points on average) which is what the orthodoxy predicts. What the orthodoxy ignores, however, is the impact of trade liberalisation on imports and the balance of payments. Trade liberalisation has invariably raised the growth of imports by more than exports, leading to balance of payments difficulties for countries, which has either constrained their growth or led to greater international indebtedness in financing the deficits. Research by

Christian Aid (2005) shows that the effect of import growth exceeding export growth as a result of trade liberalisation has cost sub-Saharan Africa $272 billion in lost output over the last 20 years; far in excess of aid, and enough to wipe out debts if aid had not been conditional on trade liberalisation. If there has been any improvement in growth performance, it has been very modest and at the expense of wider trade deficits. There is no convincing evidence that the crucial trade-off between growth and the balance of payments has improved as a result of trade liberalisation, and in the case of Latin America, as we have shown, there is strong evidence that the trade-off has worsened. We return to Rodrik's (2004) remarks in his WIDER lecture: 'Latin America of the 1990s is a region of openness, privatisation and liberalisation . . . [but] the cold fact is that per capita economic growth performance has been abysmal during the 1990s by any standards'. In fact, Rodrik examines 83 growth accelerations across the world over the period 1957–92 and finds that only 15 per cent of them were preceded by trade liberalisation, and that only 18 per cent of significant liberalisations produced growth acceleration.[6]

Just as important as what has happened to aggregate growth performance in individual countries is what has happened to the international distribution of income, and the distribution of income within countries. Has trade liberalisation and increased 'globalisation' produced a fairer world economy, and a more equal distribution of income across people of the world? The next two chapters address these issues.

Notes

1. For further elaboration of these ideas and models, see McCombie and Thirlwall (1994, 1997, 2004).
2. The term '45-degree rule' was coined by Krugman (1989) but the result had already been derived by Prebisch (1959) and Thirlwall (1979). In Krugman, however, the direction of causation runs from differences in growth rates to differences in income elasticities not from differences in income elasticities to differences in growth rates. The Krugman model is fundamentally implausible for primary producing developing countries.
3. Note, however, that no impact was found from joining NAFTA in 1994.
4. Two techniques were used: first, dynamic panel estimation with (i) fixed effects and (ii) using generalised methods of moments (GMM); second, time-series/cross-section estimation for all countries, and for the countries in the four 'regions' separately.
5. There are 50 of these countries defined by UNCTAD, consisting of the poorest countries of the world.
6. A growth acceleration is defined as a growth difference of 2 percentage points or more between eight years before the event and eight years after, with a minimum post-acceleration growth rate of 3.5 per cent.

3. Trade liberalisation and international inequality

> [T]he poorest half of the world's population received less than one-tenth of the global growth in the 1990s. In fact, the 19 per cent of world population living on less than $1 a day received less than 2 per cent of the increase in global consumption. (Edward, 2006)

Facts and Orthodoxy

We live in a very divided world between rich and poor; between the 'haves' and the 'have-nots'. By any measure one cares to take, the evidence is unequivocal that the world's income is distributed extremely unequally between nations and people. The World Bank classifies the countries of the world into three broad categories: low-income, middle-income and high-income countries. In 2005, the average level of per capita income in the low-income countries, containing 2.4 billion people, was US$580, compared to US$35 000 for the high-income countries containing one billion people. This gives a relative income gap between rich and poor countries of approximately 60:1. The relative income gap between rich and poor people, of course, is much higher. If the income per head of the poorest countries (roughly $100 per head in Burundi and Ethiopia) is compared with the richest countries such as Norway, Switzerland and the United States, the relative gap is approximately 600:1. And, if the income per capita of the poorest people in poor countries is compared with the income per head of the richest people in rich countries, the gap becomes colossal. The richest 1 per cent of people in the world receive as much income as the poorest 60 per cent. The 50 million richest people in the world receive more total income than the poorest three billion. The total income of the richest 25 million Americans alone is more than the total income of the poorest two billion in the world. The assets of the world's 400 dollar billionaires (mostly resident in rich countries) exceed the total income of nearly one-half of the world's total population. Forty per cent of the world's population lives on less than $1000 per annum, or $2.73 per day. It is no wonder that the United Nations Development Programme (1997) has described the world as 'gargantuan in its excesses and grotesque in its economic and human inequalities'. There are nearly 2.5 billion people in the world living in absolute poverty on less than US$2 per day; and nearly one billion suffer various forms of malnutrition and illness, living on the equivalent of less than US$1 per day. If the world's population is divided up into equal 20 per cent shares from poorest to richest, and the percentage of income received by each share is shown graphically, the picture, ironically, resembles a champagne glass with a very narrow stem in the hands of the poor and a wide open bowl (containing the champagne, of course) in the hands of the rich (Wade, 2001).

But according to orthodox growth and trade theory, the world should not be like this. Orthodox neoclassical growth theory (Solow, 1956), which is still widely taught to economics students across the world, predicts that levels of per capita income should converge across countries. Because of the assumption that additions to capital (investment) are subject to diminishing returns, the marginal product of capital in poor (capital scarce) countries should be higher than in rich countries, so that if tastes and preferences for consumption and saving are the same across countries, poor countries should grow faster than rich countries, leading to a convergence process. Unfortunately, however, none of the assumptions of neoclassical growth theory bear any relation to reality. Savings and investment ratios are *not* the same across countries and capital is not subject to diminishing returns because in the real world such factors as education, research and development, and even trade keep the marginal product of capital from falling. This is formally recognised in so-called 'new' growth theory, or endogenous growth theory, but there is still the presumption in these new models of what is called beta (β) convergence, or conditional convergence; that is, there would be convergence if levels of investment, education, research and development, and so on were the same across countries. This is little comfort, however, to poor countries that cannot afford to save or to spend on education and research. 'Catch-up' theories of growth also predict convergence. Poor, backward, countries should be able to catch up with technological leaders by borrowing technology without having to invest in producing technology themselves. One of the mechanisms by which this can happen is by foreign direct investment and trade. But poorer countries have to possess the capabilities and institutional structures to absorb the technology (Abramovitz, 1986).

Orthodox trade theory likewise teaches that trade should be equalising. It is true that there is nothing in the doctrine of comparative advantage which says that the total resource gains from trade will necessarily be equally distributed between trading partners – this depends on the relationship between the external rate of exchange for commodities and the internal rate of exchange – but certainly the Heckscher–Ohlin theorem and Samuelson's factor price equalisation theorem predicts that returns to factors of production, and especially wages, will equalise across countries. But the evidence does not support the theorem, as we shall show in Chapter 4.

Non-Orthodox Models of Divergence

In contrast to orthodox theory, there is a rich body of non-orthodox theory that predicts the possibility of economic divergence between countries, regions and people depending on the economic and institutional structure and environment in which people live and work. Those who are not orthodox in the neoclassical sense, and are not obsessed with the notion that everything in the economic and social system must tend towards equilibrium, have never been surprised to see vast differences in the distribution of income and wealth across countries and peoples, and that they have grown historically through time. John Stuart Mill (1848), one of the pioneers of trade theory over 150 years ago, was aware of the possibility that some countries may get locked into activities with an inherently low growth potential, such as primary production, while others produce and trade more sophisticated goods. There are the cumulative causation and centre–periphery models of Myrdal (1957), Hirschman (1958), Prebisch (1950, 1959) and Singer (1950), recently rediscovered and re-modelled by the so-called 'new' economic geography (Krugman 1991, 1995). Then there is the powerful Marxist literature on unequal exchange, and the exploitation of poor countries by rich through dependency and multinational investment (for example, Emmanuel, 1972; Amin, 1974; Frank, 1967) which some would argue has lost none of its relevance. It is important to briefly review these non-equilibrium models before trying to disentangle the evidence on whether trade liberalisation has decreased or increased the degree of global inequality we observe today. If the orthodoxy is right, we should be optimistic; but if the non-orthodox models are based on more realistic assumptions, the prospect for a fairer world, left to market forces, is bleak.

Gunnar Myrdal, the famous Swedish economist and winner of the Nobel Prize for Economics in 1974, was among the first in the post-war era to challenge in a systematic way the notion that if income differences arise between regions or countries, economic and social forces will come into play to narrow and eliminate those differences (Myrdal, 1957). On the contrary, he argues that the neoclassical mechanisms of labour migration, capital mobility and trade are likely to perpetuate or even widen differences once they arise, unless there is appropriate State intervention. To illustrate what Myrdal has in mind, consider two regions at an equal level of development, and then assume that one of the regions (A) experiences a favourable exogenous shock which makes it richer than the other region (B), and reduces unemployment there too. Neoclassical theory argues that labour will migrate from B to A to take advantage of the difference in economic opportunities, and that this shift in labour supply will cause incomes and unemployment to equalise. But this is a very static view of the world. Labour migration not only changes labour supply in the two regions but also labour demand, because the demand for goods and services will tend to fall in the region of out-migration and rise in the more prosperous region. The demand for labour moves in the same direction as the supply for labour, keeping differences in income levels and unemployment the same. Labour migration is also a selective process leading to a loss of human capital in the poorer region, and an equivalent gain in the richer region. This will tend to lead to widening disparities.

Now consider the flow of capital. In neoclassical theory, capital should flow to the poorer region where the wage rate is lower because this is supposed to be where the profit rate is higher. But this is also a static view. Apart from the fact that an inverse relation between the wage rate and profit rate across regions is not guaranteed, entrepreneurs take investment decisions on the basis of expected returns in the future. They invest in markets and locations where demand is buoyant, not in regions from which people are migrating. On balance, capital is likely to flow from poor to richer regions, widening further the disparity in economic performance. Finally, trade between the regions is also likely to be disequilibrating, particularly if the favoured region (A) receives its initial boost from the production and export of a new manufactured good produced under conditions of increasing returns. In these circumstances, success will breed further success because as the demand for the good increases, costs will fall making the good even more competitive. The disadvantaged region will find it difficult to compete without protection or exceptional industrial enterprise. Myrdal refers to this perpetuation and widening of differences between regions as a process of 'circular and cumulative causation', in which the favoured regions have so-called 'backwash effects' on other regions, reinforcing their initial advantage. Rich regions can have some favourable 'spread effects' on poorer regions, such as the transfer of technology and the provision of infrastructure, but they are generally weaker than the 'backwash effects'.

Myrdal believed that the same forces that operate at the regional level also work at the international level to perpetuate and widen differences in the level of development between countries. International labour migration is not equilibrating because it tends to be skilled and qualified labour that migrates from poor to rich countries, while the flow of unskilled labour from poor to rich countries (which might be Pareto optimal) is tightly controlled. International capital does not flow primarily to poor countries where wages are lowest, but to richer countries where market demand is higher. The exception to this rule is poor countries which are growing fast where not just the money wage, but also the efficiency wage (that is the money wage relative to labour productivity), is low; for example China, which absorbs over one-half of foreign direct investment (FDI) that flows to developing countries. By contrast, Africa, containing the poorest countries in the world, receives hardly any FDI except in the oil and mineral sectors. Finally, international trade is not equalising because of the nature of the goods produced and exported by rich and poor countries. As long as poor countries specialise in primary products, the gains from trade will always accrue largely to the rich countries producing goods with more favourable production and demand characteristics.

The distinguished development economist, Albert Hirschman, argues in the same vein as Myrdal in his classic book, *Strategy of Economic Development*, published one year after Myrdal's. Hirschman refers to the forces perpetuating differences between regions and countries as 'polarisation effects', which are essentially the same as Myrdal's 'backwash effects'. In the context of regions within a country, Hirschman suggests that poorer regions might be better off if they became sovereign states, or at least were provided with some of the equivalents of sovereignty. If a lagging region became an independent country, it would be easier to control the mobility of factors of production; competition between the lagging region and richer region could be reduced; forms of protection could be implemented, and the lagging region could even adopt its own exchange rate. Some former 'regions' of the world have recently become independent states, as in the former Yugoslavia and USSR, and now prosper.

The 'new' economic geography, pioneered by Krugman (1991, 1995), builds on the insights of Myrdal and Hirschman, and also attempts to explain why some regions become rich and others poor in terms of what are called 'centripetal forces' which lead to industrial concentration in favoured (rich) regions, and 'centrifugal forces' which lead to industrial dispersal, giving a more even distribution of income across regions. In contrast to

Myrdal and Hirschman, however, distance and transport costs play a key role. There is always a tug of war going on between centripetal forces which promote geographic concentration of activities, and centrifugal forces that oppose it. The centripetal forces, acting as magnets for activity, are mainly different types of external economies associated with the size of markets and linkages between activities, labour market externalities (for example pools of skilled labour) and price externalities, such as knowledge spillovers. The centrifugal forces, resisting concentration, are such factors as the immobility of factors of production, higher rents in concentrated areas and pure external diseconomies, such as congestion costs. Within this framework, the emergence of a 'centre' and 'periphery', and shifts in the regional pattern of development, can be explained in terms of the changing balance between the pull of the market on the one hand and transport costs on the other.

As with Myrdal's model, consider first of all identical regions. If transport costs are very high, each region will be more or less self-sufficient. Activity, including manufacturing, will be widely dispersed serving local markets because it is too costly to transport inputs and output elsewhere. Now suppose that transport costs start to fall. It becomes more economical for some regions to supply the needs of others. Those regions with some small initial advantage, as a result of geography or historical accident, will tend to capitalise on that advantage, exporting manufactures to the less favoured regions and driving out business there. Activity becomes concentrated in a core (or centre), leaving a run-down periphery with agriculture or petty service-type activities. Small initial differences between regions become magnified through the forces of cumulative causation based on increasing returns associated particularly with market size (agglomeration economies). The periphery, however, will tend to have relatively low production costs, particularly low wage costs because of large reserves of labour. At some point, if transport costs fall even more, it may become economical to shift production from the centre to the periphery because low production costs now outweigh the cost of transport to the market. This is the main explanation of why, in recent years, there has been a major shift in the world's manufacturing base from the 'centre' of Europe and North America to the 'periphery' of South East Asia, and especially China. These mechanisms outlined above help to explain the evolution of divisions between regions and countries in the world which can spontaneously emerge with better communications, and then go into reverse when transport costs fall even lower (Krugman and Venables, 1995). It is not, however, an equilibrium world; it is an ever-changing world in which economic development in some regions or countries may be precluded altogether. It is no surprise that Africa has some of the poorest and most stagnant economies in the world. Geography and transport are stacked against it.

The Argentinian economist, Raul Prebisch (1901–86), who was Director of the Economic Commission for Latin America (ECLAC) from 1948 to 1964, and the first Secretary General of UNCTAD established in 1964, was the first modern critic of the view that trade between regions or countries is necessarily mutually beneficial as mainstream trade theory argues. While orthodox trade theory measures the benefits of trade by the saving of real resources that countries gain from specialising in what they are best at producing, Prebisch (1950, 1959) focused on the monetary consequences of trade – neglected by traditional theory – namely the effect that patterns of trade have on the balance of payments and terms of trade. If the structure of trade leads to one set of regions or countries running balance of payments deficits, while others run surpluses, and the only way for deficits to be corrected is to slow the growth of output to reduce the growth of imports, then relative income differences are bound to arise between regions or countries (see Chapter 2, p. 69). The potential real resource gains from trade are offset in the deficit country by the underutilisation of resources. This is a classic 'centre–periphery' model based on the structural characteristics of production and trade. For Prebisch, the solution was for the periphery to protect itself; to substitute imports for domestic production, and to make the 'periphery' more like the 'centre'. Latin America pursued the import substitution route to development between the 1950s and the 1970s, largely under Prebisch's influence, with some degree of success, at least compared to the post-trade liberalisation experience since the 1980s (although not compared with the more export-oriented economies of South East Asia).

Prebisch also pointed out the adverse effect that a particular structure of production and trade can have on the terms of trade of a country; that is, on the price of its exports relative to imports. Countries producing and exporting primary commodities, for example, may be at a disadvantage because the demand for these commodities tends to grow slower than for manufactured goods (Engel's Law), and cost reductions are not passed on to workers in the form of higher wages because there is surplus labour and labour has no bargaining power. Thus, both the forces of demand and supply keep the price of primary commodities down relative to manufactured goods, over the long run. Prebisch (1950) originally suggested an average historical deterioration of the terms of trade of primary commodities of 0.9 per cent per annum between 1876 and 1939. Work by Hans Singer (1950) at the United Nations also indicated a trend deterioration over the same period, but at a slightly slower rate of 0.64 per cent per annum. The Prebisch–Singer thesis of the deteriorating terms of trade for primary commodities was born, and subsequently spawned a huge literature which has largely confirmed the thesis. The terms of trade for primary commodities relative to manufactures is not the same, of course, as the terms of trade of developing countries relative to developed countries because the former countries export some manufactures and the latter export some primary commodities. But all the research shows, however, not only a decline in the terms of trade of primary commodities over the last hundred years or more of roughly 1 per cent per annum (Cashin and McDermott, 2002), but also a decline in the terms of trade of developing countries because the price of their low value-added manufactured exports tends to fall relative to the price of manufactured exports of developed countries. Poor developing countries suffer double jeopardy. The deterioration of the terms of trade for many poor developing countries accelerated in the 1980s as they were forced to liberalise under World Bank/IMF Structural Adjustment Programmes, and as they tried to export their way out of the debt crisis that had engulfed them. An outward shift of a supply curve along an inelastic demand curve which is shifting outwards only slowly is a recipe for terms of trade deterioration. For a country exporting and importing, say, 40 per cent of its GDP, and experiencing a 2 per cent per annum deterioration in its terms of trade, it will suffer a 0.8 percent (0.4 × 2 per cent) reduction in its real income growth per annum below what it would otherwise be. This is a substantial loss for a poor country caused by dependence on the export of primary raw materials which serve as inputs into the processed goods of industrialised developed countries.

This leads us to the various theories and models in the Marxist tradition, concerned with dependency, exploitation and unequal exchange, which also predict divergence in the world economy. A part of the dependency and unequal exchange relation between 'centre' and 'periphery' is related to the characteristics of trade, as described above in the models of Prebisch and Singer, but there are many other important dimensions to the argument, such as: the dependence of the periphery on foreign capital, and the expropriation of the surplus (or profit) by the centre; the dependence on foreign technology; mechanisms that reduce real wages in developing countries below what they would otherwise be, and various socio-cultural aspects of neo-colonialism that thwart the drive for independence and self-reliance. Writers in the Marxist tradition, such as Dos Santos (1970), Frank (1967), Amin (1974) and Emmanuel (1972) argue that unequal development must be viewed as an integral outcome of the functioning of the world capitalist system. The major source of income inequality is the inequality of wages between rich and poor countries which is the basis of Emmanuel's theory of unequal exchange. Exchange is unequal between rich and poor countries because wages are lower in poor countries, and lower than if the rate of profit in poor countries was not as high as in rich countries. In other words, exchange is unequal in relation to a situation in which wages would be equalised: 'Inequality in wages as such, all other things being equal, is alone the cause of the inequality of exchange'. Low wages suit the capitalists in poor countries, and suit the developed countries that import their goods. One of the ways of keeping wages low in surplus labour economies is to keep labour productivity low in agriculture because the agricultural wage determines the industrial wage. As Arthur Lewis (1954) remarked in his classic paper on 'Economic Development with Unlimited Supplies of Labour': 'the record of every imperial power in Africa has been one of impoverishing the agricultural sector'.

Emmanuel's argument is essentially a terms of trade argument which, as we have seen, has some force. For other Marxist writers, inequality is inevitable because the development of some countries implies the distorted development or underdevelopment of others. Development itself perpetuates underdevelopment, a process that Frank has called 'the development of underdevelopment'. The origins of this process go back to colonialism which started as a form of economic exploitation and has distorted the economic structure of developing countries ever since. The developing countries were forced into the position of being suppliers of raw materials to industrial countries, thus effectively blocking industrial development in the primary producing countries themselves. Recall the way that Britain tried to stifle industrial development in its colonies in the 18th century, as we outlined in Chapter 1. This is colonial dependence, based on trade and the exploitation of natural resources, but other forms of dependence developed which still thwart the development process in poor countries. One is financial-industrial dependence which consolidated itself at the end of the 19th century, and effectively geared the economic structure of developing countries to the needs of the 'centre'. Rich countries organised the banking sector of poor countries for their own profit. Another form of dependence is technological-industrial, which emerged after the Second World War based on multinational corporations which began to invest in industries geared to the internal market of developing countries, and to repatriate their profits back to the 'centre'. Dos Santos (1970) argues that each of these forms of dependence has so conditioned the internal structure of peripheral countries that this itself has become part of the dependency relation: for example, the highly dualistic structure of poor countries; the income inequality and conspicuous consumption of the wealthy classes; a dependency mentality and the ingrained habit of seeking outside help, and the alliance between the domestic ruling elite and foreign interests all conspire to impede internal development. In other words, dependency is not simply an external phenomenon, it also has to do with supportive power groups within the poor countries themselves which find the status quo profitable.

Measures of Inequality and Historical Trends

In the debate over what has been happening to inequality in the world economy over time, and particularly in the era of trade liberalisation which started in developed countries in the 1950s, and in the majority of developing countries in the 1980s and 1990s, there are three measures or concepts of inequality that need clearly distinguishing: firstly, international inequality, with each country treated as a single unit and given equal weight in the measure; secondly, international inequality with each country treated as a single unit but weighted by its size of population; and thirdly, global or world inequality which takes the individual person (not the country) as the unit of measurement, and therefore takes account not only of differences in income between countries, but also between people within countries. Each measure has its own purpose, and there is no theoretical reason why the measures should move together (although, in practice, they tend to, taking a long historical perspective).

There are many different indices that can be used to measure the extent of inequality. There is the absolute gap (or range) between the richest and poorest country; the relative gap between richest and poorest, or the variation of countries' income around the mean level of income for all countries, measured by the variance (or log variance), the standard deviation (the square root of the variance) or the coefficient of variation (the standard deviation divided by the mean of the sample). But the most commonly used integral measure of inequality in most studies is the Gini ratio which lies between zero and one, and is constructed on the

basis of the distribution of income across countries
or people, represented on a diagram by a Lorenz
curve. We will describe below how this is constructed, but it needs to be said in advance that a
single statistic, such as the Gini ratio, does not say
what is happening *within* the distribution, and in
particular, what is happening at the extremes of the
distribution. Ratios of extremes, such as the income
of the poorest 10 per cent of the world's population
compared to the richest 10 per cent, or income of
the poorest countries compared to the richest, says
as much if not more about inequality and social
justice than any integral measure. In fact, the Gini
ratio may indicate convergence or less inequality,
while the ratio of extremes is increasing. Later on,
therefore, we will supplement the research on the
Gini ratio with alternative measures of distribution
and inequality.

Consider now Figure 3.1. On the vertical axis is
measured the percentage of income, and on the
horizontal axis is measured the percentage of population. To draw the distribution of income (the
Lorenz curve) first rank each country, groups of
countries, or groups of individuals in ascending
order according to the ratio of the percentage of
income they receive and the percentage of population they represent; then cumulate the observations, and plot them on the diagram. To give a
simple example, suppose we take the World
Bank's division of countries into low income,
middle income and high income, and that low-
income countries contain 40 per cent of the world's

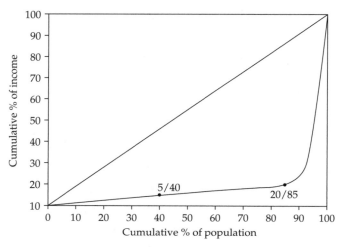

Figure 3.1   Lorenz curve diagram

population and receive only 5 per cent of world income; middle-income countries contain 45 per cent of the world's population and receive 15 per cent of world income, and high-income countries contain 15 per cent of the world's population and receive 80 per cent of world income. The cumulative distribution of income in relation to population would then be 5/40; then 20/85 (when middle-income country figures are added), and finally 100/100 when the high-income countries are added. These points are plotted in Figure 3.1, and the curve joining them is the Lorenz curve. The diagonal 45-degree line on the diagram shows an equal distribution of income. The position of the Lorenz curve in relation to the 45-degree line therefore gives a visual impression of the degree of inequality. The closer the Lorenz curve, the more equal the distribution, and the more 'bowed' the

curve the more unequal the distribution. The Gini
ratio is calculated as the area between the Lorenz
curve and the 45-degree line divided by the area of
the triangle it lies within. If the Lorenz curve is
coincident with the 45-degree line, the Gini coefficient would be zero – complete equality. If one
person received all the world's income, the Lorenz
curve would follow the horizontal and vertical
axes and the Gini coefficient would be one.

When we examine international and global
inequality, what we shall find is that through time,
at least since the early 1900s, the Lorenz curve has
been shifting outwards, and the Gini ratio has
been rising, although according to some investigators it may recently have levelled off, albeit at a
high level. A central estimate for the current level
of international inequality would be a Gini ratio of
0.55, and for a global inequality a Gini ratio of
0.65. But, as we shall come to see, estimates vary
depending on such factors as the sample of countries taken; how income is measured – whether by
per capita income or household income – and
whether income is measured in US$ at official
exchange rates or at purchasing power parity rates
(PPP). What is clear from the outset, however, is
that if trade is an equalising force its impact must
have been offset by more powerful forces leading
to inequality, otherwise the Gini ratios would not
have risen so high. For the moment, we will not try
to isolate the independent effect of trade; merely
document the historical and contemporary evidence. We shall rely on three major studies. The

first is by Milanovic (2005b) who uses 360 household income and expenditure surveys within countries for the years 1988, 1993 and 1998. The second is by Bourguignon and Morrisson (2002) who take 33 countries (and groups of countries) going back to 1820 using data on per capita income and the distribution of income from Maddison (1995). The third is by Sala-i-Martin (2002a) who combines individual income distributions for 125 countries between 1970 and 1996, covering nearly 90 per cent of the world's population.

International Inequality (Unweighted and Weighted)

The unweighted Gini ratio of international inequality takes each country as one unit, regardless of population size, and assumes that each person within the country has the same average income. The distribution of income within the country is not considered. It is countries that are the focus, not people. The ratio is basically, therefore, a measure of whether or not countries are converging with each other, not whether the distribution of income across individuals in the world is becoming more or less equal. What does the evidence show? Using the best historical data available (Maddison, 2001; Bourguignon and Morrisson, 2002) for 26 countries covering nearly 80 per cent of the world's population, the Gini ratio in 1820 was approximately 0.2. This is very low by current standards. Two hundred years ago, international differences in income per head were not great. Maddison (1995) shows that the ratio of per capita income of the richest to the poorest country in 1820 was only 3:1, compared to nearly 600:1 today.

Table 3.1 shows the evolution of the unweighted Gini ratio through time, rising consistently to 0.54 in 2000 – a more than doubling of income inequality in the space of nearly 200 years. Some of the increase may be spurious due to the larger sample of countries used to calculate the index, but Milanovic shows that for the same 26 countries as used for the 1820 calculations, the Gini ratio still rises to just over 0.5 in 2000. For the period since the Second World War, when trade liberalisation started in earnest, the Gini ratio shows an increase for a consistent set of over 100 countries from 0.45 in 1952 to 0.54 in 2000; an increase of 20 per cent. There is no evidence of declining international inequality; that poor countries have grown faster on average than rich countries. On the contrary, they have been growing slower. This was particularly true after the oil shock of 1979, with the tripling of interest rates, the catastrophic fall of commodity prices in the early 1980s, and the onset of the international debt crisis which hit Latin American and African countries particularly hard. Ghose (2004) takes a sample of 76 developing countries and 20 developed countries over the period 1981–97, and finds that the Gini ratio rose at a rate of 0.4 per cent per annum. Inequality has not only increased between countries of the world

Table 3.1 A comparison of Gini ratios

| Year | International Inequality[1] | | Global (or World) Inequality | | |
	Unweighted	Population weighted	Milanovic (2005b)	Bourguignon and Morrisson (2002)	Sala-i-Martin (2002a)
1820	0.20	0.12		0.50	
1870	0.29	0.26		0.56	
1890	0.31	0.30		0.59	
1913	0.37	0.37		0.61	
1929	0.35	0.40		0.62	
1938	0.35	0.40			
1952	0.45	0.57		0.64	
1960	0.46	0.55		0.64	
1978	0.47	0.54		0.66	0.66 (1970)
1988	0.50	0.53	0.62		0.65
1993	0.53	0.52	0.65	0.66 (1992)	0.64
1998	–	–	0.64		0.63
2000	0.54	0.50			0.63

Source: [1] Adapted from Milanovic (2005b), Table 11.1.

but also between countries in the poorest continents of the world of Africa, Asia, and Latin America and the Caribbean. Between 1960 and 2000, the Gini ratio rose in Africa from 0.38 to 0.51, in Asia from 0.36 to 0.53, and in Latin America and the Caribbean from 0.31 to 0.35. Only the richest countries of Western Europe, North America and Oceania show a decrease in inequality with the Gini ratio falling from 0.23 to 0.16. All this is consistent with what we know from tests for convergence using 'new' neoclassical growth theory. For example, simply regressing the growth of per capita of countries on the initial level of per capita income shows no negative relation (for example, Barro, 1991; Pritchett, 1997; Ghose, 2004), which is a necessary condition for convergence, but there is evidence of 'convergence clubs' (for example, the convergence of per capita incomes within the countries of the European Union). There is evidence for conditional convergence across countries of the world; that is, there would be convergence if levels of savings and investment, education and R&D expenditure were the same across countries, but this is hardly a comfort to poor countries that want to catch up. These growth variables are exactly the ingredients of faster growth that they lack. The fact is that the rich countries have tightened their grip on the income generated by the world, and only a handful of countries in recent years have made it to the rich man's table such as Singapore, Hong Kong, Taiwan, South Korea and Malaysia. Countries with the highest per capita income in the mid-19th century are still today's richest countries.

Turning now to the weighted measure of international inequality, Table 3.1 tells a slightly different story. It shows the Gini ratio peaking in 1952 at 0.57 and declining to 0.50 in 2000. This implies that poor countries with large populations must have been growing faster on average than richer countries with smaller populations. In the 1950s and 1960s this was due to the fast growth of some of the big Latin American countries, such as Brazil and Mexico, and of Japan and South Korea, all using trade protection of one form or another. In the 1980s and 1990s the decline in the weighted Gini ratio has been largely due to the rapid growth of a small number of poor populous Asian countries, especially India and China. Ghose (2004), in his study of 96 countries over the period 1981–97, finds that the weighted Gini ratio fell by 0.7 per cent per annum, but only 17 of the 76 developing countries in the sample converged on the per capita income of the 20 developed countries. The majority of poor developing countries diverged. Despite the fall in the ratio since 1952, it is still high and much higher than the estimate of 0.12 in 1820. In other words, for a large part of the last two centuries, the world's poorest and most populous countries have fared badly compared with the smaller, rich countries of the world. China and India are now reversing the trend, but their recent rapid economic growth is based more on domestic economic reform and the growth of exports, than on free trade.

Global (or World) Inequality

The Gini ratio of global (or world) inequality takes into account not only differences in average per capita income between countries, but also differences in income per capita within countries. Because internal income distributions are never equal, the measure of global inequality is bound to be higher than the unweighted measure of international inequality. It also means that changes in the global distribution of income are an amalgam of forces including: what is happening to the distribution of income between countries; what is happening to population growth in rich and poor countries; and what is happening to the distribution of income within countries. What does the evidence show? As far as the historical record is concerned, Bourguignon and Morrisson (2002) have tried to measure inequality among world citizens back to 1820 using a sample of 33 countries (or groups of countries) and measuring domestic income inequality by taking decile income shares (with the top decile of income earners divided into two). The results are shown in Table 3.1. It can be seen that the global Gini ratio in 1820 was already 0.5, more than double the level of international inequality, implying that domestic inequality was as great, if not greater, than international inequality. Through time, global inequality has increased, but as a result of rising international inequality, not because of even greater inequality within countries. On the contrary, income inequality in many countries shows a decrease historically, particularly in the richer countries of the world (the inverted Kuznets curve). Bourguignon and Morrisson calculate that within-country inequality accounted for 80 per cent of global inequality in the first half of the 19th century, when most countries were more or less at the same income level, but by 1950 within-country inequality accounted for only 40 per cent of global inequality because of the increase in inequality between countries. Today, the figure is about 20 per cent. The Gini ratio of global inequality seems to peak in the late 1970s at 0.66, and has more or less stayed stable since then. At least the changes look minor compared to the unequivocal increase since 1820. But conflicting forces are still at work. International inequality is still increasing, but at a slower rate than in the past because of the fast growth of China and India; income distribution within some countries is narrowing, but in China and India the income distribution is widening particularly between the rural and urban sectors. This is probably now the greatest force preventing a fall in the global distribution of income.

Sala-i-Martin (2002a) covers the more recent period from 1970 to 1998 taking the income distribution of 125 countries and aggregating them. Despite the much larger sample, the calculated global Gini ratios are remarkably similar to those of Bourguignon and Morrisson. The estimate for 1970 is 0.66 (see Table 3.1), gradually falling to 0.63 in 1998. The explanation for the slight fall is that the lower 'tail' of the aggregated income distribution has shifted rightwards more dramatically than the upper 'tail', largely due to developments in China and India. Fast growth in these two countries has lifted millions of people above the $1 a day poverty line, and has reduced the relative income gap with richer countries, and this has been enough to just offset the worsening income distribution within China and India, as mentioned earlier. Still, we have evidence again of global inequality on a vast scale which persists despite the massive growth world trade.

Milanovic (2005b) has also undertaken the Herculean task of bringing together 360 household sample surveys of income and expenditure for nearly 100 countries for the years 1988, 1993 and 1998, covering 80–90 per cent of the world's population. There are 86 countries with samples for all three years, containing 84 per cent of the world's population. For this common sample of countries, the calculated global Gini ratio using household income or expenditure measured at purchasing power parity (PPP) is 0.62 in 1988, 0.65 in 1993 and 0.64 in 1998. For the full sample of countries (102 in 1988, 121 in 1993 and 122 in 1998) the Gini ratios are exactly the same as for the common sample. These estimates are remarkably similar to those of Sala-i-Martin, despite the difference in samples, and the measure of income. The mean income or expenditure from household surveys will be less than per capita income (or GDP per head) because the former excludes taxes and the provision of public goods. Nonetheless, Milanovic shows that if all survey incomes are scaled up by the ratio between GDP per capita and the survey mean, the Gini ratios hardly differ: 0.64 in 1988, 0.66 in 1993 and 0.64 in 1998. Of the total global inequality estimated, between 70 and 80 per cent is attributed to differences in the mean income between countries, leaving the minor part to be explained by inequality within countries. These results are confirmed by Edward (2006) using national consumption distributions and collating them into a global distribution measured at PPP in US$ for 1993 and 2001. The global Gini ratio is estimated at 0.610 for 1993 and 0.614 for 2001. Just over 80 per cent of this inequality is the result of between-country differences.

As was said at the beginning, however, the Gini ratio does not indicate what is happening at the extremes of the distribution. Also, nothing has been said about the performance of the 'continents' in which developing countries are located. Table 3.2 from Sutcliffe (2004) rectifies this omission. The first two rows give the coefficient of variation of per capita income for years since 1950, and the ratio of average income per head of the ten richest countries to the ten poorest. The coefficient of variation shows a decline in inequality over the whole period, but it is concentrated in the years 1950–80 when the developing countries were growing relatively fast. Since 1980, in the most intense period of trade liberalisation, the coefficient of variation has increased slightly. This

Table 3.2 *Alternative measures of inequality*

	1950	1955	1960	1965	1970	1975	1980	1985	1990	1995	2001
Coefficient of variation of GNP per capita at PPP (145–163 countries)[1]	1.59	1.54	1.43	1.23	1.22	1.12	1.06	1.01	1.06		
									1.00	1.07	1.08
Ratio of average GDP per capita of 10 richest countries to 10 poorest countries	36.2	35.8	33.9	31.7	32.7	32.0	32.2	30.1	34.2	39.2	47.0
Average income as per cent of developed countries:											
Less-developed countries	19.3	18.5	18.6	17.0	16.2	16.4	15.9	15.3	14.5	14.6	15.0
Africa	15.8	14.4	13.6	12.5	11.7	10.9	10.3	8.9	7.7	6.8	6.6
Latin America	44.4	40.9	40.4	35.7	34.2	36.0	36.1	30.7	26.9	27.5	25.8
Asia	11.2	11.0	10.9	9.7	9.5	9.9	10.0	10.8	11.3	13.5	14.5

Note: [1] The break in the series in 1990 is due to the division of the former USSR, Yugoslavia and Czechoslovakia.

Source: Sutcliffe (2004).

increase in inequality is shown even more dramatically by the rise in the ratio of per capita income in the ten richest countries to the ten poorest from 32 in 1980 to 47 in 2001.

Table 3.2 also shows the average per capita income in the major continents of the world compared to the developed countries. In less-developed countries as a whole the ratio has fallen from 19.3 per cent to 15 per cent. Only in Asia has the ratio risen, from 11.2 to 14.5 per cent – but still the ratio is very low. In Africa and Latin America, the ratio has plummeted, especially in the last 20 years. This is evidence of divergence, not convergence. These are the facts. Now let us turn to studies which explicitly attempt to assess the role of trade, and whether trade liberalisation has been an equalising or disequilibrating force.

The Impact of Trade Liberalisation on Inequality

One methodological approach to the issue of whether or not trade liberalisation has contributed to rising international inequality is to interact a measure of trade openness with the level of per capita income to see whether the impact of openness varies with the level of development. Do poor countries benefit more than the rich, or vice versa? This is the approach of Dowrick and Golley (2004) who take over 100 countries and two separate periods, 1960–80 and 1980–2000, and regress the growth of per capita income on: (i) trade as a percentage of GDP (as a measure of openness); (ii) an interaction term of trade openness and a country's level of per capita income; (iii) a dummy variable to capture specialisation in primary production, and (iv) a number of other control variables. They also run separate regressions for developed and less-developed countries. The results are revealing. For the first period, 1960–80, taking 117 countries, a higher trade share of 1 percentage point is associated with 0.11 per cent faster growth, and the poorer the country, the slightly greater the benefit from openness. This would be evidence of trade leading to convergence. These results, however, do not carry over to the period of increased liberalisation, 1980–2000, where the impact of the trade share is now negative (−0.072) and the interaction term with the level of per capita income is positive (+0.009) indicating that rich countries benefited from trade more than the poor, leading, by itself, to divergence. Dividing the sample from 1980–2000 into 33 less-developed countries and 78 developed countries shows no significant effect of an increase in the trade share on growth in the poorer countries, while the richer countries gained by about 0.012 percentage points for a one percentage point increase in the trade share. Dowrick and Golley conclude: 'trade has promoted strong divergence in productivity [per capita income] since 1980'. Specialisation in primary production (measured by more than a 50 per cent share of exports) had no significant effect on income growth in the 1960–80 period, but had a strong negative effect in the period 1980–2000, reducing per capita income growth on average by 0.8 percentage points. The negative impact is even stronger within the less-developed country group, producing a growth difference of −1.76 per cent. If one of the major beneficial effects of trade is to enable countries to access technology, this is a fairly clear indication that countries specialising in primary production find it difficult to adopt new (superior) technology, either because they do not need it or lack the capability to absorb it. The difference in the impact of trade in developing countries between the periods 1960–80 and 1980–2000 may have to do with the change in the nature of technology transfer. Pre-1980, the transfer of technology involved mostly knowledge and capital goods required for well-established manufacturing processes that developing countries found easy to adopt, whereas post-1980 technology has become more complex (for example, information and communication technologies), which many poor countries do not have the requisite infrastructure and human capital to use.

Another methodological approach to the relation between trade and international inequality is to examine what happens to the dispersion of per capita income between countries pre- and post-liberalisation, or what happens to the dispersion of income between countries that liberalise and those that do not. In this vein, Parikh and Shibata (2007) examine 64 developing countries over the period 1970–99, of which 40 liberalised during the period:

9 in Asia, 15 in Africa and 16 in Latin America. In each of these regions they test for beta and sigma convergence before and after liberalisation.[1] They find no evidence of unconditional beta convergence either before or after liberalisation. On the other hand, taking the standard deviation of the natural logarithm of the per capita income of countries in each region (the test for sigma convergence), and regressing on time, with a shift and slope dummy variable for the years of liberalisation, shows evidence of convergence in Asia and Latin America post-liberalisation, but increasing divergence in Africa. The issue of divergence with the richer, developed countries, however, is not addressed.

The only other major study in this field that attempts to answer the question of whether trade liberalisation has contributed to international inequality is by Ghose (2004) who takes 96 countries over the period 1981–97, and examines the relationship between the rate of change of the trade/GDP ratio (as a measure of trade liberalisation) and both the level of per capita income in 1981 (measured at PPP) and the size of population. Overall, he finds that the effect of trade liberalisation on trade performance has been much the same for poor and rich countries, and that, therefore, trade liberalisation has had no discernable effect on international inequality, unweighted by population size. On the other hand, there seems to be a positive relationship between trade performance and population size. Since populous countries are mostly low-income countries, Ghose conjectures that trade performance may have contributed to the decline in the population-weighted Gini ratio discussed earlier. No doubt, however, this result is heavily influenced by India and China, the two most populous countries in the world, both of which started with a very low trade base in 1981. In both cases, however, export growth has been the driving force, not trade liberalisation, and the two processes should not be confused.

Conclusions

From the evidence available, we conclude that there is no rigorous scientific evidence that the process of trade liberalisation in the last 30 years or so has led to greater income equality across countries of the world. If anything, controlling for the size of countries, poorer countries seem to have benefited less than richer countries since the process of liberalisation accelerated in the 1980s. What is happening in the world economy as liberalisation continues apace is that rich countries, plus India, China and a few other 'favoured' countries, are forging ahead, while the vast bulk of poorer countries are languishing in their wake. This portrait more closely mirrors the predictions of non-orthodox trade and growth theory than orthodox models of trade and growth which predict convergence. The world resembles more the 'cumulative causation' model of Gunnar Myrdal and others, than the equilibrium world of the neoclassical mainstream.

To summarise what has been happening to international inequality against this background of trade liberalisation and expanding trade, we can do no better than repeat the six propositions of the distinguished development economist, Robert Wade, in a powerful essay written in 2004:[2]

Proposition 1: World income has become rapidly more unequal when incomes are measured at market exchange rates, and expressed in US$.

Proposition 2: World PPP–income polarisation has increased, with polarisation measured as the ratio of income between the richest and poorest deciles.

Proposition 3: Between-country world PPP inequality has increased since at least 1980, using per capita GDPs, equal weights, and a coefficient like the Gini ratio for measuring the whole distribution.

Proposition 4: Between-country world PPP income inequality has been constant or falling since around 1980, with countries weighted by population size [but this is entirely due to the high weights of India and China].

Proposition 5: Several serious studies find that world [global] PPP–income inequality has increased within the past two or three decades, taking account of both between- and within-country distributions.

Proposition 6: Pay inequality within countries was stable or declining from the early 1960s to

1980–82, then sharply increased to the present. 1980–82 is a turning point toward greater inequality in manufacturing pay worldwide.

We look at proposition 6 in more detail in the next chapter on trade liberalisation and income inequality within countries. What we can be sure about in the years ahead, however, is that whatever happens to relative inequality, the absolute gap between the richest and poorest countries will continue to widen, with all the implications this has for political tensions in the world, conflict, international migration and the smouldering sense of injustice between the 'haves' and 'have-nots'. Even if poor countries with an average per capita income of US$1000 were to grow at 6 per cent per annum (which is high) compared to 1 per cent per annum (which is low) in rich countries with per capita income of US$30 000, the absolute gap in income would continue to grow for 40 years, and would not be eliminated for over 150 years (Wade, 2004).[3] This is some measure of the divided world in which we live.

Notes

1. Beta (β) convergence refers to the sign of the relationship between the growth of per capita income and the initial level of per capita income. A negative sign would indicate convergence. Sigma (σ) convergence refers to the standard deviation of per capita income.
2. Updated in 2008, Wade (2008).
3. See Thirlwall (2006) for how to make these calculations.

4. Trade liberalisation, poverty and domestic inequality

> While inequality has many different dimensions, all existing measures for inequality in developing countries seem to point to an increase in inequality which in some cases . . . is severe. (Goldberg and Pavcnik, 2007)

Introduction

There may be static efficiency gains from trade liberalisation and a greater volume of trade, but there will also be welfare losses if domestic firms cannot compete as trade barriers fall and those thrown out of work cannot find alternative employment. Just as the distribution of gains from trade may not be equally spread between trading nations, so, too, the gains from trade to a country may not be equally distributed between people within a country, and some may lose absolutely. If more trade leads to faster economic growth, this should lift more people out of poverty and reduce the poverty rate, depending on the elasticity of the poverty ratio with respect to growth. However, as we saw in the previous chapter, trade liberalisation is no guarantee of more rapid economic growth, and even if the poverty ratio declines the income distribution may still become more unequal, if the richest in a country gain relatively to the poorest. These are the issues that we shall consider in this chapter: what has been the impact of trade liberalisation on poverty, on wage inequality and on the personal distribution of income within countries? These are important issues because poverty and inequality matter for the humane and efficient functioning of societies and economies. Poverty and inequality tends to be associated with higher unemployment, poor health, crime and lower standards of public service which all affect the quality of life. Unequal societies also tend to have weaker property rights for the ordinary citizen and more fragile democracies which impair the development process.

Poverty

First of all, we need to mention briefly the various links and channels through which trade liberalisation might affect the level of poverty, however the poverty level is defined. It is useful for empirical purposes to distinguish the two main groups in society that receive a country's real income: workers (or wage earners) on the one hand, and producers (or profit earners) on the other. In the latter category are included not only firms and enterprises, but also the self-employed who are consumers as well as producers, such as peasant farmers in rural areas, and those eking out a living in the petty service sector of the urban areas of developing countries. Wage earners will be affected by trade liberalisation in three main ways: by what happens to the wage rate, to employment and to the price of goods they consume. There are many possibilities. If liberalisation increases productivity, and real wages rise, workers will benefit. If labour supply is perfectly elastic, however, wages will not rise and any gains in productivity will accrue to employers. Wages may fall if domestic industries are threatened with increased competition from abroad. Indeed, this is the greatest loss likely to be suffered by workers; the loss of jobs in import-competing activities, which means lower employment and lower wages.

In Kenya, both cotton farming and textile production have been badly affected by trade liberalisation. Cotton production fell by 70 per cent between the mid-1980s and mid-1990s, and employment in textile factories fell from 120 000 to 85 000 in ten years (Christian Aid, 2005). The maize growers of Mexico have suffered badly from the 1994 NAFTA agreement because they cannot compete with the heavily subsidised maize from the US. On the other hand, export industries should benefit from trade liberalisation, providing more employment and higher wages. Workers will also benefit if the prices of the consumption basket that they buy falls. Price changes will have distributional effects depending on the weight of each good in each worker's basket. If the price of food falls, the poor will gain more than the rich because the poor spend a higher proportion of their income on food. If liberalisation raises the price of food, however, because of the removal of subsidies, for example, the poor are likely to suffer severely. What happens to the welfare of workers, therefore, depends on a multitude of circumstances. Undoubtedly, some will gain and some will lose depending on the activities that have been protected; how domestic industry responds to the challenge of greater competition; the response of the export sector to new opportunities, and what happens to the prices of various goods.

Producers will also be affected in a variety of ways, in particular by what happens to output prices; to input prices, and to the prices of the basket of goods bought for consumption in the case of self-employed producers. Producer prices are likely to fall with trade liberalisation. In Senegal, after liberalisation, the price farmers received for their tomatoes fell 50 per cent, and tomato production fell by 70 per cent, leaving many farmers without a cash crop (Christian Aid, 2005). But the price of imported inputs is also likely to fall. Whether producers gain or lose will depend on the prevailing protective structure of their output and inputs. If a producer goes out of business, there is, or course, a total loss of income (including wages). There are also macroeconomic considerations to bear in mind. It is sometimes argued that trade liberalisation makes economies more vulnerable to shocks, because they are more open, which may have the effect of increasing poverty when economic conditions are adverse. Similarly, the impact that liberalisation has on government revenue and expenditure will also affect the poor. One serious effect of cutting tariffs is that it reduces government revenue, which may result in less spending on projects that help the poor, including infrastructure and welfare spending.

If any generalisation can be made from case studies it seems that when all price and wage effects are taken into account, rural families tend to lose, and urban households tend to gain – at least in circumstances where workers retain their jobs. Ravallion (2006) concludes, on the basis of his micro case studies of trade liberalisation in China and Morocco, that 'the most vulnerable households tend to be rural dependent on agriculture, with relatively few workers, and with weak links to the outside economy through migration'. We do not concur with the conclusion of Winters et al. (2004) in their survey of trade liberalisation and poverty when they say:

> [t]heory provides a strong presumption that trade liberalisation will be poverty-alleviating in the long run and on average. The empirical evidence broadly supports this view and, in particular, lends no support to the position that trade liberalisation generally has an adverse impact. Equally, however, it does not assert that . . . the static and micro-economic effects of liberalisation will always be beneficial to the poor. Trade liberalisation necessarily implies distributional changes; it may well reduce the well-being of some people (at least in the short term) and some of these may be poor. (pp. 106–7)

Economic theory does *not* predict that trade liberalisation is poverty alleviating; all it predicts is static efficiency gains. It says nothing definite about long-run growth, or about the distribution of the gains from trade between countries. What we shall see below is that in the greatest era of trade liberalisation since the early 1980s, the absolute number of poor people in the world, outside of China, has actually *increased*, which is not a good advertisement for a doctrine which proponents of liberalisation claim will spread prosperity to all.

The latest comprehensive studies on absolute poverty, and the effect of trade on poverty, are by Chen and Ravallion (2004), Edward (2006) and Ravallion (2006). First of all, let us give the facts on the level of poverty by the standard criteria of the numbers of people living on less than US$1 and US$2 a day. Chen and Ravallion use household survey data covering 454 surveys in 97 countries over the period 1981–2001, and find that the number living on less than US$1 a day declined by nearly 400 million, while the number living on less than US$2 a day increased by nearly 300 million. The estimated drop in the number living on less than US$1 a day is much greater than previous estimates, including those of the World Bank (2002), but the whole of the decline is accounted for by China where poverty fell by 422 million. Table 4.1 gives the figures for the major regions of the world in 1981, 1990 and 2001.

Excluding China, those living in extreme poverty on less than US$1 a day increased by 22 million from 848 million in 1981 to 870 million in 2001. Or taking the US$2 a day criterion, the world's absolute poor outside China increased by 567

Table 4.1   Absolute poverty and poverty rates, 1981–2001

Region	Absolute Poverty (millions)						Poverty rate (%)					
	$1 a day			$2 a day			$1 a day			$2 a day		
	1981	1990	2001	1981	1990	2001	1981	1990	2001	1981	1990	2001
East Asia	795.6	472.2	271.3	1169.8	1116.3	864.3	57.7	29.6	14.9	84.4	69.9	47.4
China	633.7	374.8	211.6	875.8	824.6	593.6	63.8	33.0	16.6	88.1	72.6	46.7
E. Europe and Central Asia	3.1	2.3	17.0	20.2	22.9	93.3	0.7	0.5	3.6	4.7	4.9	19.7
Latin America and the Caribbean	35.6	49.3	49.8	98.9	124.6	128.2	9.7	11.3	9.5	26.9	28.4	24.5
Middle East and N. Africa	9.1	5.5	7.1	51.9	50.9	69.8	5.1	2.3	2.4	28.9	21.4	23.2
South Asia	474.8	462.3	431.1	821.1	957.5	1063.7	51.5	41.3	31.3	89.1	85.5	77.2
India	382.4	357.4	358.6	630.0	731.4	826.0	54.4	42.1	34.7	89.6	86.1	79.9
Sub-Saharan Africa	163.6	226.8	312.7	287.9	381.6	516.0	41.6	44.6	46.4	73.3	75.0	76.6
Total	1481.8	1218.5	1082.0	2450.0	2653.8	2735.4	40.4	27.9	21.1	66.7	60.8	52.9
Total excluding China	848.1	843.7	870.4	1574.2	1829.2	2141.8	31.7	26.1	22.5	58.8	56.6	54.9

Source: Chen and Ravallion (2004).

million. It is true that the poverty *rate* for people on less than $1 a day has fallen, even excluding China, but the poverty rate for those on less than US$2 a day, excluding China, has hardly changed in 20 years of pro-liberal domestic and international economic policymaking. The rate was 58.8 per cent in 1981 and 54.9 per cent in 2001. The situation in Africa is particularly serious, where the number in poverty has doubled, and the poverty rate has increased as well. Over 75 per cent of the population live on less than US$2 a day. In Latin America and the Caribbean, the number of poor people has also increased and the poverty rate has remained unchanged, despite (or some would say, because of) two decades of liberal economic reforms. Edward (2006) confirms the results of Chen and Ravallion. Using consumption data from household surveys, he estimates a fall in US$1 a day poverty from around 1.2 billion in 1993 to 1.1 billion in 2001, but all the fall is accounted for by China. Outside of China, the number living on less than US$1 a day increased. The number living on less than US$2 a day stayed roughly the same at 2.7 billion.

Turning now to the effect of trade liberalisation on the rate of poverty, Ravallion (2006) first takes 75 countries where there have been at least two household surveys on poverty (178 cases in all), and runs a simple regression of the percentage change in the poverty rate on the percentage change in the ratio of trade to GDP. No relation is found. He then takes the same 75 countries and the longest spell between surveys in each of the countries, and runs the same regression. There is now a statistically significant negative coefficient of 0.84, but the correlation is very fragile. For example, controlling for initial conditions turns the relation insignificant, and adding other control variables makes no difference. Ravallion concludes 'it remains clear that there is considerable variation in the rates of poverty reduction at a given rate of expansion of trade volume'. But how about China? Is greater trade openness the cause of the dramatic fall in the poverty rate there? Ravallion examines the time-series data for China over the period 1980–2000, and finds no robust relationship. Cointegration tests reject the hypothesis of a long-run relationship between changes in the trade share and changes in the poverty rate. In any case, most of the poverty reduction in China came in the early 1980s as a result of agricultural reforms, before more liberal export-orientated trade policies were implemented. Overall, Ravallion concludes his study of trade and poverty reduction across countries by saying: 'based on the data available from cross-country comparisons, it is hard to maintain the view that expanding trade is, in general, a powerful force for poverty reduction in developing countries'.

Wages and Income Inequality

We turn now to the issue of the impact of trade liberalisation on wage and income inequality within countries, which is not necessarily the same as the impact on poverty or the poverty rate. Poverty can fall but wage and income inequality can rise because the share of income going to the top income recipients (of both wages and other income) rises by more than the share going to the bottom. In general, what will happen to the income distribution as trade liberalisation takes place will depend on how the wage distribution is affected, how the distribution of assets changes and what happens to the rate of return on assets.

As far as wage inequality is concerned, orthodox trade theory predicts that as trade liberalisation takes place there should be a narrowing of the gap between skilled and unskilled wages in poor countries and a widening of the gap in rich countries. As we saw in Chapter 1, according to the Heckscher–Ohlin theorem, countries will benefit by specialising in the production of those goods which use their most abundant factor of production. Poor countries with abundant labour and scarce capital should specialise in labour-intensive goods using relatively unskilled labour. The Stolper–Samuelson theorem then says that the relative wages of skilled and unskilled labour is determined by the relative price of goods. The removal of tariffs in poor countries should reduce the price of 'skilled goods' and reduce the wage of skilled labour relative to unskilled labour leading to convergence, while the removal of tariffs in rich countries should reduce the price of 'unskilled goods' and reduce the wages of unskilled labour relative to skilled labour leading to divergence.

The evidence from a variety of sources, however, does not support the prediction of either of these theorems for poor developing countries. Wage inequality, and the gap between skilled and unskilled wages (the skill premium, as it is sometimes called), has been widening in the vast majority of countries, not diminishing. Also, there is little evidence that labour in poor countries has been reallocated from skill-intensive to less skill-intensive products, or that the share of unskilled labour in most industries has risen; rather, the opposite. The explanation is that the assumptions of the traditional, orthodox models are far too restrictive to capture what is going on in the real world. Apart from the usual free market assumptions of perfect competition and the free mobility of capital and labour within countries, there are also the extremely restrictive assumptions of fixed technology, only two factors of production, and no factor flows of capital or labour between countries. This is serious because the process of trade liberalisation that the world has witnessed over the last 30 years or so has also been accompanied by the massive liberalisation of factor flows between countries, including substantial foreign direct investment in poor countries, increased labour mobility between countries (skilled and unskilled) and the intensive exploitation of land-based natural resources (a third factor of production). On top of this, there is a continual bias in technical progress taking place against unskilled workers. These facts not only make it difficult to test directly the impact of trade liberalisation on wage inequality, but make it almost certain that growing wage inequality will be found as a worldwide phenomenon, and not just in rich, developed countries. First let us consider some of the empirical evidence, and then offer some of the competing hypotheses which upset the predictions of the Heckscher–Ohlin and Stolper–Samuelson theorems for poor developing countries.

Robbins (1996), Freeman and Oostendrop (2001), Zhu and Trefler (2005), Anderson (2005), Goldberg and Pavcnik (2007), and Vos et al. (2002) all give extensive evidence of a worldwide trend towards greater wage inequality between skilled and unskilled labour in poor countries.[1] Robbins (1996) uses data on hourly wages of salaried employees from household surveys in Argentina, Chile, Colombia, Costa Rica, Malaysia, Mexico, Philippines, Uruguay and Taipei, and finds that, except in Taipei, trade liberalisation raised the relative wage of skilled workers compared to unskilled. The author's explanation is the increased import of capital goods into poor countries, which he calls the skill-enhancing trade hypothesis (see later). Freeman and Oostendrop (2001) construct consistent data on the relative wages of production workers (mainly craft workers, operators and labourers) compared to non-production workers (mainly managers, professional technicians and clerks) in 20 developing and newly-industrialised countries in the 1990s, and find that in more than half of the countries there is evidence of rising inequality. They find no correlation between changes in inequality and the level of per capita income, as predicted by the Heckscher–Ohlin and Stolper–Samuelson theorems. Zhu and Trefler (2005) use the Freeman–Oostendrop data set and find a strong correlation across countries and over time between the skilled/unskilled wage differential and the shift in the export share of poor countries towards more skill-intensive goods. The authors call this the 'catch-up' hypothesis (see later). Vos et al. (2002) conclude their extensive study of trade liberalisation in Latin America by saying:

> virtually without exception, wage differentials between skilled and unskilled workers rose in the post-liberalisation period. In a number of cases there were widening income differentials between formal and informal sector workers . . . [because] excess labour was typically absorbed in the non-traded, informal trade and service sectors (as in Bolivia, Colombia, Costa Rica, Ecuador, Panama and Peru), or in some cases traditional agriculture served as a sponge for the labour market (Panama in the late 1980s, Guatemala and Mexico). (pp. 12, 15)

Goldberg and Pavcnik (2007), in their comprehensive survey of the distributional effects of globalisation in developing countries, focus on Mexico, Colombia, Argentina, Brazil, Chile, India and Hong Kong during the 1980s and 1990s. These are countries that underwent drastic trade liberalisation during these years, for which there is reliable data before, during and after liberalisation. It is found that all the countries seem to have experienced an increase in the skill premium whether measured by the ratio of wages of non-production workers to production workers, or by the rate of return to higher education (investment in skills). Also the Gini ratio of wage dispersion is shown to have risen. The authors have no doubt that the major cause of the rise in the skill premium is the rise in the demand for skilled labour, but caution against attributing it all to 'pure' trade liberalisation because of a variety of other changes going on domestically and in the world economy, such as privatisation, labour market reforms and foreign direct investment flows. To know how much changing wage inequality is due to trade liberalisation and how much to other factors requires 'strong modelling and identifying assumptions'. One possibility in this regard is to examine the relative wages of skilled and unskilled labour in different industries or occupations *within* a country where industries have been affected differently by tariff cuts and other forms of trade liberalisation.

As well as wide-scale cross-country studies of wage movements, there have also been many individual time-series case studies. Anderson (2005) surveys 14 time-series studies of the effect of openness on the relative wage of skilled labour across a broad cross-section of developing countries, and concludes that although there is some evidence to support orthodox theory in a small number of countries in South East Asia, the major overall finding of most studies is that 'reductions in barriers to trade and foreign investment increase the relative demand for skilled labour either by shifting the structure of production towards more skill-intensive sectors or by increasing the use of foreign, skilled biased, technologies by individual firms and enterprises'. In other words, trade liberalisation, in general, increases wage inequality. Important individual case studies include those of Feenstra and Hanson (1997) and Hanson and Harrison (1999) for Mexico, and Arbache et al. (2004) for Brazil. In the case of Mexico, where wage inequality has increased markedly since the trade liberalisation was embarked on in the mid-1980s, Feenstra and Hanson develop the 'outsourcing' hypothesis for the increase in the skill premium (see below), while Hanson and Harrison point out that prior to trade reforms in Mexico, the labour-intensive sector was the most heavily protected, so that if the tariff on unskilled labour-intensive goods fell by more than on skill-intensive goods, this would also raise the relative wage of skilled labour. Brazil started serious trade liberalisation in 1991, and Arbache et al. show that rates of return to college education increased, rates of return to the lowest four educational levels fell, and wage inequality rose – driven partly by falling real wages in the traded sector (through increased competition) and partly by skill-enhancing trade associated with inflows of foreign direct investment.

These last observations lead us on to a more detailed, systematic statement of the various hypotheses that have been advanced to explain rising wage inequality in poor countries, contrary to the prediction of orthodox theory. Some of the hypotheses or explanations can be considered within the Heckscher–Ohlin, Stolper–Samuelson theoretical framework, while others lie outside. Within the orthodox framework, it makes a difference to the predictions of the model if more than two countries and two factors of production are considered. Consider first the case of one rich developed country, and two poor countries that trade with each other as well as trading with the rich country. The trade of the poorest with the least poorest may reduce the wages of unskilled labour in the latter and worsen the income distribution, even though the country is still poor relative to the rich one. For example, a poor country, such as Mexico, is caught between a poorer country, China, and the US. Theory says that trade liberalisation between Mexico and the US should narrow wage inequality, but China penetrating Mexican markets reduces unskilled wages in Mexico and increases wage inequality. With more than two countries there are conflicting forces at work. Secondly, consider the case of a third factor of production in a poor country, such as land containing natural resources, for example oil or minerals. If skilled labour is assumed to be a complement to land, and trade and trade liberalisation favours the export of land-intensive goods, this will raise the demand for skilled labour and increase wage inequality in the poor country, despite its abundance of unskilled labour. Thirdly, it must also be remembered that within the orthodox framework, the initial level of protection of different goods prior to liberalisation is not considered. The Stolper–Samuelson theorem assumes the movement from autarchy to free trade and nothing in between. However, if the most highly protected industries in poor countries prior to liberalisation are the most labour-intensive, this will keep the wage of unskilled labour high, which will then fall relative to skilled wages after liberalisation. Or, in other words, the skill premium increases instead of decreasing.

Outside of the standard orthodox framework, there are a number of other competing hypotheses to account for the rise in the skill premium in poor countries. Firstly, there is the theory developed by Feenstra and Hanson (1996, 1997) related to trade in intermediate goods, and rich developed countries shifting the production of inputs to poorer countries, or outsourcing. From the rich country's point of view, these activities use relatively large amounts of unskilled labour, but from the poor country's point of view, the labour they use is relatively skilled. So, unskilled wages fall relative to skilled wages in the rich country, and skilled wages rise relative to unskilled wages in the poor country. The authors test the model with respect to US foreign direct investment in the maquiladora sector of Mexico post-liberalisation in the mid-1980s and find that in regions where FDI was most concentrated, the growth of FDI accounted for over one-half of the increase in the share of skilled wages in total wages. Any foreign direct investment flows into poor countries will tend to increase the demand for skilled labour because in general there is a complementarity between new investment (particularly that embodying technical progress) and skilled labour. To the extent that trade liberalisation encourages, or is accompanied by, FDI flows, it should occasion no surprise that the predictions of the orthodox models are not met. Orthodox theory assumes that capital is immobile internationally.

A second class of theories developed to explain the widening wage gap between skilled and unskilled workers in poor countries is related to skill-biased technological change, which may be endogenous to trade liberalisation itself. There are number of different strands to the argument. Firstly, Wood (1995) argues that more competition as a result of trade liberalisation will induce firms to engage in what he calls 'defensive innovation', either taking advantage of existing new technologies or spending on research and development. This leads to the prediction that skill-biased technical change should be greatest in the industries where trade barriers fall the most, and this appears to be the case. Secondly, skill-biased technical change in poor countries could come about through the increased import of machinery with trade liberalisation, and this is what Robbins (1996) finds in his work. Thirdly, there may be the attempt by poor countries to 'catch up' with the rich through increasing their export shares of skill-intensive goods. Quality upgrading of products within an industry requires more skilled labour.

Exports may be relatively more skill-intensive than products for the domestic market, and trade liberalisation encourages more exports. This is the hypothesis of Zhu and Trefler (2005) mentioned earlier, which also bears some similarity to the 'outsourcing' model of Feenstra and Hanson (1996), who find a close association between the growth of the skilled wage premium across countries and the growth of export shares in skill-intensive products.

Wood (2002) develops a more complex model which leads to multiple outcomes, and can account for the different experience of countries, particularly between Latin America on the one hand, and some of the South East Asian countries on the other. Two different forms of trade openness are distinguished: the traditional falling barriers to trade on the one hand, and the falling costs of moving knowledge around the world on the other which enable firms in rich countries to provide technical and marketing expertise in poor countries. In rich countries there are knowledge workers (K), producing high-quality tradeable goods (A), while in poor countries there are medium-skilled workers (M) and unskilled workers (U) producing two types of goods – high-quality tradeables (A) and low-quality non-tradeables (B). All high-quality goods require the input of knowledge workers from rich countries. As travel and communication costs fall, rich countries shift more production of high-quality goods to poor countries. This induces a shift of labour out of non-tradeables. What happens to the demand for medium-skilled workers (M) relative to unskilled workers depends on whether the new production of skill-intensive goods requires a higher or lower ratio of M workers to U workers than in the non-traded sector. This process associated with the shift of knowledge alters the sectoral composition of employment in rich and poor countries. The increased supply of high-quality goods from the poor country exporter to the rich country, in particular, shifts labour out of the tradeable into the non-tradeable sector and unequivocally increases wage inequality in rich countries. In the poor country, however, the effect on relative wages depends on how much transport and communication costs fall, and on the initial conditions of the poor country. For example, if a poor country had very little human capital and produced very few high-quality goods, a fall in the cost of transferring knowledge to the poor country would raise wage inequality because activities transferred from the rich country would be more skill-intensive than those in which workers were currently employed. On the other hand, if the poorer country had a higher level of human capital, the activities shifted from the rich country may be less skill-intensive than existing production, and wage inequality would decline. Later on, activities may become more skill-intensive, increasing wage inequality again. This theory would be consistent with Wood's (1997) findings that in some East Asian countries, such as South Korea and Taipei in the 1960s, Singapore in the 1970s and Malaysia in the

1970s and 1980s, wage inequality decreased following trade liberalisation, while it increased in Latin America.

Wage differences between skilled and unskilled workers are not the only source of income inequality, although according to Goldberg and Pavcnik (2007) income inequality tends to move in the same direction as wage inequality. Greater trade openness may alter the gap in earnings between men and women; between regions within a country; between rural and urban areas, and also change the rate of return on assets, all of which will affect a measure of income inequality, such as the Gini ratio. What is the evidence?

Income Inequality and Trade Liberalisation

The evidence on income inequality within countries is that it has increased markedly in most countries in the last 25 years or so, compared to the relative stability, or even decrease in inequality, in the 1950s, 1960s and 1970s. Cornia and Kiiski (2001) examine 73 countries with time consistent information over the period of the 1950s to the 1990s, covering 80 per cent of the world's population and 90 per cent of world GDP, and find an increase in inequality, as measured by the Gini ratio, in 48 of them: 17 with a continuous pronounced rise, 29 with a rise since the 1980s and 2 with a very slight rise. Only nine countries in the sample evidenced falling inequality (for example Norway, Malaysia, Philippines and South Korea, among the biggest countries). The authors attribute the increase to 'a shift towards skill-intensive technology, and especially, to the drive towards domestic deregulation and external liberalisation'. Table 4.2 gives the Gini ratios for a selection of developing countries in the 1990s, and the latest figure available from the World Bank.[2] Gini ratios are generally higher in Latin America than in Asia or Africa, but it can be seen that in most countries in the last decade or so, inequality has continued to increase. Brazil and Venezuela are notable exceptions where deliberate income redistribution policies have been implemented to raise the income of the poor.

But what about the impact of trade liberalisation on the income distribution? Milanovic (2005a) says in his survey of income distribution studies:

> the conclusions run nearly the full gamut, from openness reducing the real income of the poor to openness raising the income of the poor proportionately less than the income of the rich to raising both the same in relative terms. *Note, however, that there are no results that show openness reducing inequality; that is, raising incomes of the poor proportionately more than the incomes of the rich – let alone raising the absolute incomes of the poor by more.* (p. 23) (Emphasis added)

The most highly publicised and 'rose tinted' view that 'growth is good for the poor', and that trade has not reduced the share of income going to the poor, is the study by Dollar and Kraay (2002, 2004). Firstly, using the Deininger and Squire (1996) data set on income inequality (consisting of Gini ratios

Table 4.2   Income inequality in selected developing countries measured by the Gini ratio

Country	Earliest date in the 1990s[1]	Latest date in the 2000s[2]
Bangladesh	28.3	33.4
Bolivia	42.0	60.1
Brazil	63.4	57.0
Chile	56.5	54.9
China	41.5	46.9
Colombia	51.3	58.6
Dominican Republic	50.5	51.6
Egypt	32.0	34.4
Ghana	33.9	40.8
Honduras	52.7	53.8
India	33.8	36.8
Indonesia	31.7	34.3
Jamaica	41.1	45.5
Mexico	50.3	46.1
Nigeria	37.5	43.7
Pakistan	31.2	30.6
Peru	44.9	52.0
Philippines	40.7	44.5
Sri Lanka	30.1	40.2
Thailand	46.2	42.0
Venezuela	53.8	48.2
Zambia	46.2	50.8

Sources:
1. World Bank, World Development Indicators 1997 Table 2.6.
2. World Bank, World Development Indicators 2007 Table 2.7.

and quintile income shares for 108 countries over the period 1947–94), they plot changes in the Gini ratio against changes in trade shares for more than 100 developed and developing countries, and find no relation. Looking at rich and poor countries separately, and using other measures of openness, the conclusion is the same. In some 'globalising' countries inequality has decreased (for example, Malaysia); in others (for example, China) it has increased. Secondly, they take 80 countries over 40 years and regress the growth of per capita income of the poorest 20 per cent of the population on the growth of average income per head. They find the relationship is one to one, that is an elasticity of unity, and that the level of openness makes no difference to the coefficient. In other words, the poorest benefit equally in the fruits of growth, and openness has no effect on distributive shares. Dollar and Kraay express some surprise that they do not find a negative effect of openness on the poor, given all the assertions and adverse publicity of the anti-globalisation movement. They do various tests of robustness and stick with their original conclusion which is that 'openness to trade increases the income of the poor to the same extent that it increases the income of the other households in society'. This is not the general consensus, however, of most other studies in this field, or the latest research of Milanovic (2005b) who is critical of the Dollar and Kraay results (see later). One direct contrary study is by Edward (2006), who uses world consumption data, and finds that for roughly one billion people between the 50th and 70th percentile of the consumption distribution, consumption hardly changed between 1993 and 2001. Among the US$2 a day poor, the ratio of their consumption growth to average growth was not 1:1 but 1:2. 'Growth is good for the poor but much better for the rich'.

Higgins and Williamson (1999) test the Kuznets hypothesis that inequality first increases with development and then decreases (the inverted U hypothesis), and add the Sachs–Warner openness dummy variable to their sample of countries over the decades of the 1960s, 1970s, 1980s and 1990s, but find it makes little difference to inequality. The sign is negative but not statistically significant.

Barro (2000), using an expanded version of the Deininger–Squire data set, and a measure of openness which takes account of population, land area and trade policy, finds that trade openness increases income inequality up to a per capita income level of US$13 000 (at 1985 prices) and then decreases it.

Spilimbergo et al. (1999) use 320 observations for 34 countries and relate inequality to country endowments of capital per worker; arable land per worker, and skill intensity – all relative to the world endowment of these factors – and then attempt to assess how trade openness interacts with these variables and its effect on inequality. They find, like Barro, that openness itself worsens income inequality, but the effect is diminished, the greater the endowment of land and capital. A larger endowment of skilled labour, however, exacerbates the degree of inequality. Arable land per capita apparently makes no difference.

Mbabazi et al. (2003) take a cross-section of 44 developing countries over the period 1970–95 and find no relation between openness (measured as the proportion of years open, as defined by the Sachs–Warner index) and inequality measured by the Gini ratio, controlling for initial conditions and other variables. They express scepticism, however, as to whether cross-section analysis can ever reveal very much because of the heterogeneity of data, and conclude their study by saying: 'if we achieve no more than to convince readers to interpret cross-country evidence on inequality, growth and poverty with extreme caution and to eschew generalisations based on such evidence, we would be content'.

The most comprehensive study to date, however, of the impact of trade openness on inequality, which avoids the above criticism, is by Milanovic (2005a) who uses data from household surveys which permits the analysis of income distribution by deciles of the population instead of using a synthetic measure of the income distribution, such as the Gini ratio, which hides what is going on within the income distribution. The data include 321 household surveys from 95 countries in 1988 and 113 countries in 1993 and in 1998, covering 95 per cent of world GDP and 90 per cent of the world population. Income is measured at PPP and divided into decile shares (that is each decile contains 10 per cent of individuals). Income inequality is then measured as the income of the ith decile relative to the mean level of income. For each decile, income inequality is related to trade openness measured by the ratio of total trade to GDP, and to openness interacted with the level of income (to test whether the effect of openness on inequality varies with the level of income), plus a number of control variables such as the ratio of foreign direct investment to GDP, and the level of democracy in a country (which should be associated with greater equality). A regression is run for each of the ten deciles using the same independent variables. Two striking results emerge. Firstly, increased openness reduces the income share of the bottom six deciles. Secondly, the adverse effect of openness on inequality is less the higher the level of a country's per capita income, and the turning point for the poor to benefit from increased trade is at about US$7500 at PPP. Milanovic concludes: 'openness would therefore seem to have a particularly negative impact on poor and middle income groups in poor countries – directly opposite to what would be expected from the standard Heckscher–Ohlin–Samuelson framework'.

What accounts for the difference between the pessimistic assessment of Milanovic and the optimistic assessment of Dollar and Kraay that openness has benefited the poor as much as the average person? The major reason for the difference in results lies in the measure of trade openness. Milanovic measures openness as the trade to GDP ratio, both expressed in nominal dollars. Dollar and Kraay, by contrast, adopt the unusual procedure of measuring trade in nominal (1985) dollars but GDP in international (PPP) dollars. Since GDP measured at PPP is much higher than measured in the national accounts, this considerably understates the ratio of trade to GDP for poor countries. But the income distribution is affected by income actually received, not by national income imputed by PPP exchange rate calculations. For example, in China exports as a share of GDP measured at PPP are only 7 per cent, whereas exports as a share of nominal GDP are 26 per cent, and it is the latter that affects the income distribution. Milanovic is in no doubt that:

> the poorest deciles in poor countries – those that should benefit most from increased trade according to both economic theory and the policy prescriptions of international organisations – appear to be the losers in relative terms. The case for trade as an engine of growth for the poorest of the poor is not completely undermined, however. But the case must be based on trade's impact on average incomes . . . [not] on the basis of trade's favourable or neutral impact on income distribution. (p. 41)

Conclusions

What we have revealed in this chapter is that in an era of unprecedented trade liberalisation the number of extremely poor people in the world, outside of China, living on less than US$1 a day has increased, and so, too, has the number living on less than US$2 a day – now over 2.7 billion. Trade liberalisation has made no obvious dent on world poverty. Nor has it contributed to wage or income equality across the world. Contrary to the prediction of orthodox trade theory, the wages of unskilled labour in poor countries seem to have fallen in most countries compared to skilled wages – the same as in developed countries – and driven by the same forces of trade-related skill-biased technical change. The income distribution in most developing countries, measured by the Gini ratio, has also become more unequal, and the meticulous research of Milanovic suggests that trade liberalisation has been a contributing factor because it transpires that increased trade openness has reduced the income shares of the bottom six deciles of the income distribution. The only study that claims the contrary, that trade and growth 'has been good for the poor', is the influential work of Dollar and Kraay; but Milanovic has shown that the methodology used in their study is seriously flawed. Growth and trade openness have benefited the rich much more than the poor. If the process of economic and social development is defined to embrace the goal of reducing absolute poverty and narrowing the vast inequalities of income and wealth that characterise poor countries, the role of trade liberalisation over the last 20–30 years must be regarded as disappointing, to say the least.

Notes

1. See also Galbraith and Liu (2001) on wage dispersion between industries.
2. The prime source of data on income inequality within countries is the World Income Inequality Data Base (WIID) published online by the World Bank.

5. Trade strategy for development

> The exchange of reduced policy autonomy in the South
> for improved market access in the North is a bad bargain
> where development is concerned. (Rodrik, 2001)

In the previous chapters, we have challenged the doctrine of trade liberalisation as the certain route to development for poor countries, and surveyed the empirical evidence of the impact of trade liberalisation and greater trade openness on the growth of living standards and the distribution of income between countries and peoples of the world. The picture painted is not a rosy one, particularly for the poor, and it is time to draw some policy conclusions to provide some advice for poor countries in their future struggles and negotiations with rich developed countries and international organisations pressing for further trade liberalisation and penetration of poor countries' markets, particularly in their manufacturing and service sectors.

There is no dispute that there can be *static* resource gains from trade liberalisation, but it is important to stress again that they are not continuous – they are once-for-all – and are generally small in relation to a country's GDP, averaging not more than 1 or 2 per cent. The first question that naturally arises, therefore, is: are the benefits worth the costs of disruption and the serious distributional consequences that sudden trade liberalisation can have for particular groups in society, particularly when specialisation according to comparative advantage is likely to condemn many poor developing countries to the production of primary commodities which have such unfavourable production and demand characteristics? The answer is that in most contexts countries should either wait to liberalise or liberalise very slowly, with the emphasis on exports, until they have a more diversified production structure achieved by means of an integrated industrial and trade strategy, using a judicious mix of tariffs, taxes and subsidies, combined with the use of selective credit (see later).

More significant still to remember is that there is nothing in orthodox growth theory which demonstrates conclusively that trade liberalisation will launch a country on a permanently higher *growth* path. Some free trade economists, such as Bhagwati, are honest about that. Whether the long-run growth rate rises depends on what happens to the growth of labour productivity and employment, but in the canonical Solow growth model, these variables are exogenously determined. In 'new' growth theory, which partly draws on 'old' trade theory, and its recognition of the *dynamic* gains from trade, liberalisation may raise the long-term growth rate through the transfer of technology from rich countries raising the growth of labour productivity; but equally, and often forgotten, if trade liberalisation destroys domestic industry the growth of employment may fall, leaving the growth rate unchanged or even lower. The effect of trade liberalisation on GDP growth becomes an empirical question. It transpires that the results of statistical research relating the growth of GDP or the growth of living standards to measures of trade liberalisation, or trade openness, are very fragile depending on the sample of countries taken, the time period considered, the measures of liberalisation or openness used, and the econometric method of estimation – whether time-series, cross-section, or panel data estimation which combines both time-series and cross-section observations. The cross-section evidence suggests that becoming a more liberal, open economy may, on average, raise the growth of living standards marginally by between 0.5 and 1.0 per cent per annum, provided complementary, supportive exchange rate and macroeconomic policies are pursued, but not all countries gain equally; and the time-series evidence suggests that for countries not ready, the effect of liberalisation is negative.

The nature, sequencing and credibility of liberalisation play a significant role in determining the success, or otherwise, of the liberalisation process. Dani Rodrik's considered view (who arguably is the most seasoned researcher and thinker in the field) is: 'deep trade liberalisation cannot be relied upon to deliver high rates of economic growth and therefore does not deserve the high priority it typically receives in the development strategies pushed by leading organisations' (Rodrik, 2001). Firstly, he reminds us that trade liberalisation should not be regarded as an end in itself, only as a means to an end; and that economic crises should not, in general, be blamed on illiberal trade regimes. Yet that was the prevailing orthodox view in the wake of the debt crisis in the 1980s. He castigates the economics profession for failing to distinguish between macroeconomic mismanagement and microeconomic intervention, and lays blame for economic failure and crises squarely on the former, particularly on overvalued exchange rates and excessive budget deficits (Rodrik, 1992, 1996). Yet as a reaction to the debt crisis of the 1980s, the World Bank and IMF forced countries into excessive and premature liberalisation: 'Mexico, Bolivia and Argentina, to cite some of the most distinguished examples, have undertaken more trade and financial liberalisation . . . within five years than the East Asian countries have managed in three decades' (Rodrik, 1996). It is easier in times of crisis to implement reforms, but restrictive trade and industrial policies in these countries had little to do with precipitating crises, so their reform was not a logical necessity. Indeed, trade liberalisation is not an obvious route to macroeconomic stability; on the contrary, it can make matters worse through its adverse balance of payments effects (see below).

Secondly, there is the issue of the credibility of trade reforms. If investors are going to reallocate resources out of non-tradeables and import-competing sectors into exports, they need to be sure that the trade reforms are credible and permanent. It is costly to switch sectors initially and then switch back, and there are also risks. Without credibility, trade reform may reduce investment and growth in a country. Rodrik (1992) gives several examples.

Then we come to the issue of the sequencing of trade reforms. In this respect, the important distinction needs to be made between the liberalisation of exports and the liberalisation of imports. Exports are extremely important for a developing country because they are not only a direct source of demand for a country's output, but also provide the foreign exchange to pay for the import content of the domestic components of demand; in particular, investment necessary for the development process. Many poor developing countries do not have their own capital goods sector, and import all their investment goods from abroad. They need foreign exchange to do this, and they also need to be able to pursue a low interest rate strategy in order to promote domestic investment. This is where the balance of trade (exports minus imports) becomes important because the more favourable the balance, the lower the domestic rate of interest can be to encourage domestic investment. Trade deficits generally require a higher interest rate to finance them. This was the mercantilist argument of the 16th and 17th centuries (see Thirlwall, 2003), and Keynes's (1936) later defence of Mercantilism against the attack of Adam Smith (1776) and other classical economists. Mercantilism is not necessarily protectionist; it is about getting the balance right between exports and imports so that domestic economic policy does not become subservient to foreign trade. China is sometimes described (and criticised) as a 'mercantilist country' because of its huge trade surplus, but it allows China's GDP to grow at the enviable rate of close to 10 per cent per annum, which is unprecedented in world history, or in the contemporary world economy. Fast export growth is one of the most important ingredients of economic success because it pays for imports, but export promotion is not the same as trade liberalisation because the latter involves the dismantling of barriers to imports: both tariffs and non-tariff barriers of various types. It is one thing to argue the case against anti-export bias; it is quite another to argue for the abandonment of import restrictions which help to promote structural change within poor countries and to foster infant industries. Advocates of trade liberalisation always stress the beneficial impact of trade liberalisation on export performance, but rarely focus on the other side of the coin which is the surge of imports that may result, and the negative effects that trade liberalisation can have on the balance of payments. As Stiglitz (2006) perceptively remarks:

[A]dvocates of liberalisation . . . cite statistical studies claiming that trade liberalisation enhances growth. But a careful look at the evidence shows something quite different . . . It is exports – not the removal of trade barriers – that is the driving force of growth. Studies that focus directly on the removal of trade barriers show little relationship between liberalisation and growth. The advocates of quick liberalisation tried an intellectual sleight of hand, hoping that the broad-brush discussion of the benefits of globalisation would suffice to make their case. (pp. 72–3)

Quick liberalisation leads to a flood of imports, and one of the distinctive messages of this book is that it is extremely important for poor countries to consider the balance of payments consequences of trade liberalisation because foreign exchange is the ultimate constraint on the growth of output and living standards in many contexts. There is strong empirical evidence both for developed and developing countries that long-run growth can be approximated by the growth of exports relative to the income elasticity of demand for imports, and that currency depreciation or devaluation is not an efficient balance of payments adjustment weapon (McCombie and Thirlwall, 1994, 2004). If trade liberalisation raises the income elasticity of demand for imports by more than it raises the growth of exports, the long-run sustainable growth rate of GDP will fall. This seems to have been the experience of many developing countries that have liberalised quickly, for example Mexico (Pacheco-López, 2005). The empirical evidence, from our own research and that of others (for example Santos-Paulino, 2002a, 2002b, 2004), suggests that trade liberalisation in developing countries has raised the growth of exports by about 2 percentage points on average, but it has raised the growth of imports by more, in the region of 6 percentage points, leading to a deterioration in the trade balance relative to GDP of about 2 percentage points. This can have damaging consequences for a country if foreign investors become nervous about the sustainability of the deficits, and if domestic interest rates need to be raised to attract foreign capital in order to prevent the country's currency from collapsing. What proponents of trade liberalisation need to show is that trade liberalisation improves the *trade-off* between growth and the balance of payments if faster growth is to be sustainable, but there is little evidence of this from past liberalisations, at least in Latin America (Pacheco-López and Thirlwall, 2007).[1] Trade liberalisation that promotes export growth, by reducing export taxes, simplifying administrative procedures and so on, is to be encouraged. Trade liberalisation that leads to a flood of imports, which absorbs foreign exchange, and to a deteriorating trade balance is unlikely to be growth-promoting; on the contrary, it is likely to worsen economic performance, especially if it destroys domestic industry at the same time. This, again, raises the issue of the sequencing of liberalisation – that exports need to be liberalised before imports if trade liberalisation is to be successful and deliver its promised results.

This point is effectively the same as the common sense advice that countries should not consider full-fledged trade liberalisation until they are ready and able to compete in world markets. Before imports are liberalised, the structure of production needs to be geared to exporting, not only so that foreign exchange is available to pay for imports, but also so that there are alternative employment opportunities for those who lose their jobs in the import-competing sectors. The employment effects of trade liberalisation always need to be borne in mind because one of the most crucial assumptions of the orthodox theory of trade, and the prediction of welfare gains, is that as resources are reallocated there is continuous full employment – or as Keynes put it: 'free trade . . . assumes that if you throw men out of work in one direction you re-employ them in another. As soon as that link in the chain is broken the whole of the free trade argument breaks down' (Moggridge, 1981). In other words, if the resource gains from a more efficient allocation of resources are offset by resource losses of unemployment, trade liberalisation can lead to a welfare loss. Peddlers of the doctrine of free trade conveniently forget the full employment assumption. They also forget that different export activities have different production and demand characteristics, so that the *types* of export activities encouraged by trade liberalisation are extremely important for long-run growth. Mill (1848) recognised this a long time ago, and so does 'new' trade theory (Krugman, 1986). Exports produced under conditions of increasing returns, which are income elastic in world markets, will be associated with a faster rate of growth, and produce a faster growth of living standards, than exports produced under conditions of diminishing returns with an inelastic demand. This is why it is so important to distinguish manufacturing industry from land-based activities (primary production) for understanding the relative growth performance of nations (Thirlwall, 2002), and in making policy recommendations for structural changes. Trade liberalisation needs to be combined with an industrial strategy to foster export activities with a high growth potential in world markets. Export promotion based on primary products is unlikely to benefit economies in the long run. This is one reason why forms of protection may be necessary, both to diversify industry and promote exports at the same time, such as selective credit, subsidies to output, tax concessions on imported inputs into exports, or reduced tax on profits earned from exports. If foreign exchange is scarce, the social benefit of exports exceeds the private benefit. That is why Little and Mirrlees (1974) use saving in foreign exchange as the numeraire for the cost–benefit analysis of public projects in developing countries.

Hausmann and Rodrik (2003) add another dimension to this argument which they call the promotion of 'self discovery'. They observe that some of the most successful countries in this era of globalisation, such as South Korea, Taiwan, India and China, retained high levels of protection for a long time and made active use of industrial policies: 'the fact that the world's most successful economies during the last few decades prospered doing things that are most commonly associated with failure [e.g. protection] is something that cannot easily be dismissed'. They focus on the neglected topic of how countries encourage and promote 'learning what one is good at producing'. Making the right investment decisions is crucial for a country's growth performance, but there is much randomness in the process of a country discovering what it is good at producing. Countries can discover, often by accident, that they are good at making certain commodities at low cost such as hats, toys, footballs, and so on, but the initial entrepreneur who has the idea or makes the 'discovery' needs encouragement and 'protection' because he or she cannot appropriate the full social value that the new knowledge generates. Such discoveries are not easily patentable, and others can easily imitate. A lack of 'protection' reduces the incentive to invest in discovering what a country is good at producing. As Hausmann and Rodrik say 'laissez-faire cannot be the optimal solution under these circumstances' (just as it is not the optimal solution in the case of research and development expenditure in new processes and products which confer externalities). The authors contrast the experiences of Asia and Latin America. In Asia, governments have provided 'rents to entrepreneurs through trade protection, temporary monopolies, tax incentives, subsidies, etc. while in Latin America, the encouragement to invest in non-traditional activities has been neglected'. Trade reforms themselves are not enough to spur investment in new activities. In the theoretical model presented by Hausmann and Rodrik, however, the government, or social planner, walks a tightrope between not providing enough monopoly profit to encourage the necessary diversification and providing too much so that there is overinvestment and too much diversification. Governments must therefore use both 'carrots' and 'sticks'. The 'carrots' are the incentives, and the 'sticks' are needed to discipline those new firms that end up with high costs. Industries need to be rationalised ex-post so that there is not too much diversification.

This is where economics becomes an art as well as a science. The empirical evidence for this intriguing idea is that the resource endowment of countries is not a good predictor or explanation of what countries produce. Labour-abundant countries, such as most developing countries, have thousands of things that they could produce, yet they export only a narrow range. At an aggregate level, patterns of production may look similar at the same stage of development, but at a disaggregated level, the pattern is very different and exports are highly concentrated. Sometimes, over 70 per cent of exports are accounted for by less than ten products. Bangladesh and Pakistan are countries at similar levels of development, but Bangladesh specialises in hats and Pakistan in bed sheets. This specialisation is not the result of resource endowment; it is the result of chance choices be enterprising entrepreneurs who 'discovered' (ex-post) where costs were low. The establishment of the garment industry in Bangladesh was a speculative investment by Bangladeshi entrepreneurs in conjunction with Daewoo in Korea. No-one expected the venture to be successful, but it was, and imitation was very rapid. Other 'chance' investments include cut flowers in Colombia for export to North America; camel cheese in Mauritania for export to the EU, and high-yield maize in Malawi. The policy implications of the Hausmann–Rodrik model are that 'governments need to encourage entrepreneurship and investment in new activities ex-ante, but push out unproductive firms and sectors ex-post'. Intervention needs to discriminate as far as possible between innovators and imitators. Trade protection is not the ideal policy instrument because it does not discriminate, and increases profits only for those selling in the domestic market. Export subsidies avoid anti-export bias, but still do not discriminate between the innovators and the copycat, and in any case are illegal under the rules of the WTO. The first-best policy which can discriminate in favour of the innovator, and be used as a 'stick' if firms do not perform well, is public sector credit or guarantees.

Most poor countries (including the least developed countries) are now liberalised to a greater or lesser extent, but even where they are attracting foreign capital and increasing exports, they are not advancing technologically. Their economies remain largely dependent on primary commodities and low-skill manufacturing. Poor developing countries cannot expect to be at the frontiers of technology, but one of the arguments for trade liberalisation is that it should encourage the flow of knowledge from rich to poor countries, leading to new process and product innovation. Such innovation, potentially, is at the heart of economic diversification, technological upgrading and faster productivity growth. Unfortunately, as the *Least Developed Countries Report 2007* (UNCTAD, 2007) shows, such transfers are extremely limited, and the spillovers are minimal. It is also the case that virtually all imported technology has to be adapted to local conditions and this requires considerable time, investment and experimentation. The process of technological 'catch-up' by poor countries is one of the great challenges of development.

The different production and demand characteristics of goods produced and exported by countries is undoubtedly one of the major reasons why trade liberalisation and the process of globalisation has not been associated with any narrowing of the world distribution of income over the last 30 years. The Gini ratio for global inequality remains stubbornly high at over 0.6. Only a handful of low-income countries have matched the performance of the rich developed countries (Ghose, 2004) because the majority of poor countries still specialise in the production of primary commodities or low value-added manufactured goods. The countries that have managed to reduce the gap in living standards relative to rich countries are those that have diversified production into much higher value-added manufactured goods with increasing returns and high income elasticities of demand in world markets. These countries, mainly in South East Asia, have done so through policies of export promotion and import substitution using a combination of selective credit, subsidies and tariffs. It is not trade liberalisation that has produced success in Japan, South Korea, Taiwan, Singapore and now China and Vietnam, but domestic economic policy and strategic trade protection. Without structural change in a wider grouping of poor countries, combined with reforms of the trading rules that govern the relation between rich and poor countries (see later), the rich countries will continue to get richer and the poor countries to get relatively poorer, perpetuating or even widening the current distribution of world income.

Trade liberalisation in the last 30 years also seems to have been associated with a worsening of the distribution of income *within* countries. The major cause of the unequal distribution of global income is the unequal distribution of income *between* countries, but *within* countries there has been a widening of the distribution of income, largely associated with a widening wage gap between skilled and unskilled workers. This is contrary to the prediction of orthodox trade theory, but as we argued in Chapter 4, the standard Heckscher–Ohlin–Samuelson theory of factor price equalisation is far too limited in its scope and assumptions to capture reality; particularly its neglect of flows of FDI that often accompany trade liberalisation, and the competition *between* poor countries themselves. The flow of FDI into liberalising countries increases the demand for skilled labour, while import competition and the need for poor countries to deflate their economies to protect their balance of payments reduces the demand for unskilled labour. Certain groups of workers seem to have suffered particularly badly, especially in the agricultural sector of poor countries, and in nascent domestic industries not able to compete with foreign competition. In agriculture, the subsidy and protective policies of the European Union and the United States have seriously damaged the livelihood of many poor farmers in poor countries.

If trade liberalisation is about development, and sharing the potential gains from trade, the process needs to pay much more attention to its impact on the poor. As UNCTAD argues in its *Least Developed Countries Report 2004*, (UNCTAD, 2004),[2] trade policy should not be confused with development policy. Trade is just one aspect of development, and trade can take place without development in any meaningful sense. An exclusive focus on trade integration through liberalisation, which assumes that poverty is reduced through more trade rather than through more *development*, is likely to prove ineffective. It is necessary to look at the relationship between trade and poverty from a development perspective so that, to quote UNCTAD, 'national and international policies [are] rooted in a development-centred approach to trade rather than a trade-centred approach to development'. What is important for poverty reduction is that trade makes people more fully and productively employed, but trade liberalisation does not, and cannot, guarantee this. As we argue above, more liberal trade for developing countries may simply reinforce a vicious circle of commodity dependence with all that this implies for a slow growth of exports, terms of trade instability and decline, mounting international debt, and a lack of investment dynamism in new areas of activity. Development implies structural change, but liberal trade by itself does not guarantee the diversification of economic activity.

What is also interesting and revealing is that in the Poverty Reduction Strategy Papers (PRSPs) that poor countries must prepare to qualify for debt relief from the IMF and World Bank, there is a disconnect between the discussion of poverty and the discussion of trade. Only a few country PRSPs contain a section on trade, and where they do there tends to be merely a list of trade objectives rather than a discussion of how trade can be used to reduce poverty. Oxfam (2002) reviewed twelve PRSPs and found that only four mentioned the impact that trade reforms might have on poor people, and only two said anything about measures to protect losers. To prevent trade liberalisation from increasing poverty, at least the potential losers from trade reforms need to be identified in advance and compensatory mechanisms put in place. The World Bank and IMF have a role to play here. Instead of merely insisting on trade liberalisation as a condition of development assistance, irrespective of the consequences, it could use the opportunity of PRSPs to require all countries to include a detailed analysis of the likely effects of trade liberalisation on poverty and the domestic income distribution, and what compensation might be required. If poverty reduction is the central aim, at least of the World Bank, this is something positive and constructive it could pursue. Arguing for greater wage flexibility in poor countries, as the World Bank often does, to mitigate the negative employment effects of trade liberalisation (when wages are already pitifully low) is not only heartless, but may also prove fruitless for good Keynesian reasons. Wages are both a cost of production but also a component of demand. Cutting wages cuts the cost of production but also the demand for output. An increase in aggregate employment from money wage cuts can never be guaranteed.

'Aid for Trade' (AfT) is also a policy that could be developed further by international organisations and by the Paris Club of bilateral donors to poor countries to increase both the quantity and quality of exports. Donors could use AfT to meet the promised aid targets of 0.7 per cent of GDP, and target aid to boosting export growth in both traditional and non-traditional exports. The WTO defines AfT as comprising 'trade policy and regulations, trade development, economic infra-structure, building productive capacity and trade-related adjustment' (as quoted in Suwa-Eisenmann and Verdier, 2007). In 2005, the various forms of AfT available to poor countries amounted to $26 billion, with the vast bulk committed to economic infrastructure, and much less to trade promotion, including trade finance. Trade-related infrastructure is important to reduce the costs of storage and transportation to market. Targeted investment in roads and railways linking the agricultural hinterland to coastal ports could yield high returns by reducing transaction costs. To increase the quality of exports, and to promote structural change, aid could be used for skill training and to assist the flow of technology transfer for the production of new, higher value-added commodities identified by countries as a component of an industrial strategy; to promote 'self-discovery' (Hausmann and Rodrik, 2003). The Integrated Framework for Trade-Related Technical Assistance to Least Developed Countries (IF) launched by six multilateral organisations in 1996, and enhanced in 2005, had this in mind: first to integrate trade into national development plans (for example PRSPs), and secondly to assist trade-related technical assistance. But so far, very little has been achieved. One of the problems is that it operates in a very fragmented way. It is mostly donor-driven and lacks local ownership. Evidence also suggests that if AfT is to be successful it must be complemented by market access, otherwise attempts to diversify trade may be thwarted. To raise both the quantity and quality of exports, credit and technical assistance for the establishment of new markets also plays a vital and important role. At present, the World Bank bases its allocation of 'soft' loans from the International Development Association (IDA) on whether a country is 'liberalised' or not. One of the major components of its 'Country Policy and Institutional Assessment Score' is a country's trade policy. A top mark of 5 is given to countries where the average tariff rate is less than 10 per cent, where the sectoral dispersion of tariffs is low, and where there is no anti-export bias. In other words, a top mark is given to countries which have many of the characteristics that *prevent* countries acquiring new comparative advantage and moving up the value chain to produce higher value-added goods with more favourable production and demand characteristics.

The whole of the world trading system works against the majority of poor developing countries, firstly because of their dependence on the export of primary commodities (the 'curse' of natural resources) and low value-added manufactures; secondly, because the 'rules of the game' governing trade between rich and poor countries are rigged and biased in favour of the former, and thirdly because the agenda for trade reform is largely set by the rich developed countries. The commodity composition of trade matters for the same reasons that Prebisch (1950, 1959) outlined over 50 years ago, namely the adverse terms of trade and balance of payments effects on poor countries from the export of primary commodities and the import of manufactures. There can be no doubt about the long-run deterioration in the terms of trade of primary commodities relative to manufactured goods, or that the prices of primary products are much more volatile than the prices of manufacturers which causes a great deal of instability and hardship for poor countries. Cashin and McDermott (2002) is one of the latest of many studies to document the trend and cycles in the nominal and real prices of primary commodities over time; in their case 137 years from 1862 to 1999. Nominal prices have been very volatile around a rising trend, at least since the depths of the Great Depression in 1932. Real prices (the terms of trade) have also been volatile, but around a generally declining trend of roughly 1.3 per cent per annum. Over this period, 1862–1999, 17 non-food commodities lost 85 per cent of their real value; or, to put it another way, these commodities can now buy only roughly 20 per cent of the industrial goods that they could have bought a century or so ago. This represents a substantial loss of real income for countries where the majority of exports are primary commodities. There are, in fact, nearly 50 developing countries that depend on three or fewer commodities for more than 50 per cent of their export earnings (Thirlwall, 2006).

The estimated trend decline in the commodity terms of trade is even more pronounced if the commodity boom years of 1951 or 1973 are taken as the starting point for analysis. As far as price volatility is concerned, Cashin and McDermott find 13 occasions since 1913 when the annual price change was more than 20 per cent in one year, and conclude 'rapid, unexpected and often large movements in commodity prices are an important feature of their behaviour. Such movements can have serious consequences for the terms of trade, real income and fiscal positions of commodity-dependent countries, and have profound implications for the achievement of macroeconomic stabilisation'. Over 60 years on from Keynes's wartime proposal for a 'Commod-Control' scheme that would have limited price fluctuations within narrow (10 per cent) margins around a central price (see Thirlwall, 1987), many poor developing countries are still at the mercy of unstable commodity prices. There is a case to be made for new international commodity agreements, supervised multilaterally, and for more long-term contracts between multinational companies and commodity producers in poor countries at 'fair' prices which guarantee suppliers a living wage. This is the origin and motivation of the Fair Trade Movement founded in 1979 with the main objective of guaranteeing a price to producers above the world price with a sufficient premium above the cost of production to allow producer cooperatives to invest in community projects such as housing, health care, education and public utilities; in other words, to provide the basic needs of people (Goulet's concept of life sustenance). Unfortunately, however, the Fair Trade Movement cannot alter the fundamental forces which drive down the long-run price of primary commodities relative to the prices of manufactured goods and services. The only permanent solution to this dilemma is structural change which requires the establishment of new, non-traditional industries; and this is what the rich, developed countries are hostile to. They want free access to poor countries' markets, while continuing to protect their own. The most recent example of this is the ongoing debate between the European Union (EU) and the African, Caribbean and Pacific (ACP) countries over the Economic Partnership Agreements (EPAs) to replace the trade preferences that the ACP countries used to enjoy under the Lomé Convention, but which now fall foul of WTO rules. The EU is insisting that poor developing countries reduce restrictions on imports of manufactured goods and service activities in return for continued access to the EU market for their agricultural products. The EU is refusing to look at alternatives to free trade EPAs, but by its own admission it concedes that EPAs could lead to the collapse of the manufacturing sector in many poor countries.

This leads us on to the rules governing trade between rich and poor countries which are at present rigged against poor countries in the form of trade barriers that make it difficult for poor-country exports to penetrate rich-country markets, while pressure is put on poor countries to open up their markets to rich-country products. As Stiglitz (2006) says in his book *Making Globalization Work*, 'the United States and Europe have perfected the art of arguing for free trade while simultaneously working for trade agreements that protect themselves against imports from developing countries'. If developed countries really wanted to help poor countries, the most effective thing they could do would be to reduce tariffs and non-tariff barriers against *all* goods imported from poor countries without reciprocity and without conditions (except safety standards being met). This would simplify trade negotiations, rectify inequalities in the current trading regime, and promote development. Oxfam (2002) has estimated that trade barriers against developing countries' exports cost them more than $100 billion a year, which is twice the amount of Official Development Assistance to poor countries. It also estimates that if the developing countries could raise their share of total world exports by as little as 1 per cent, over 100 million people in poor countries would be lifted out of poverty. The policies of rich developed countries in protecting their agricultural sector are largely to blame. Agricultural support to farmers in the EU and US amounts to about $400 billion a year – nearly as much as the GDP of the whole of Africa. This support causes surpluses of commodities which are then dumped on world markets by the use of export subsidies, which, in turn, depresses the world price of these products. Some are sold at a fraction of the cost of production which destroys local markets in poor countries. At the same time, tariff barriers are erected against the import of agricultural products from poor countries. As the *International Herald Tribune* wrote (21 July 2003): 'by rigging the global trade game against farmers in developing nations, Europe, the US and Japan are essentially kicking away the ladder out from under the world's most desperate people. This is morally depraved. America's actions are harvesting poverty around the world'. It goes on to say 'the glaring credibility gap dividing the developed world's free trade talk from its market-distorting actions on agriculture cannot be allowed to continue. While nearly one billion people struggle to live on $1 a day, European Union cows net an average of $2 apiece [per day] in government subsidies'. The US spends $4 billion a year on subsidies to 25 000 cotton farmers, which profoundly affects the livelihoods of 10 million cotton farmers in countries such as Burkina Faso, Chad and Mali in West Africa. This subsidy to US cotton producers is nearly three times the US aid budget to the whole of Africa. The tragedy (and irony) is that the World Bank has encouraged these African countries to produce more cotton on the pretext of comparative advantage, but in reality they cannot compete against such subsidies. When the African countries complained at the Doha Round of WTO trade negotiations in 2002, the US Trade Representative had the audacity to tell the cotton farmers of Africa that 'they should do something else'.

Apart from the protection of agriculture, imports of textiles and garments from poor countries were also heavily restricted in the past by the Multifibre Agreement. Rich countries agreed in principle to phase out the Agreement in 2004, but in practice restrictions still exist. Of course, not only nominal protection matters, but also the protection of value-added, or the effective rate of protection, which damages the ability of poor countries to process goods and move up the value chain. The lower the nominal tariff on imported raw material inputs, and the higher the tariff on processed goods, the higher the effective rate of protection against poor countries and the possibility of ever producing the processed commodities themselves. Tariff escalation of this nature is widespread. Industries using cocoa, coffee and sugar are good examples. Oxfam (2002) has constructed a Double Standards Index measuring the gap between the free trade rhetoric of the rich countries and what they practice themselves in terms of tariffs on agricultural commodities and textiles, average tariff levels across the board, and import restrictions against poor countries, and applies it to individual countries and groups of countries. Europe comes out as the worst offender, followed closely by the US.

The rich developed countries have now instituted a form of bribe which reads: 'we will reduce agricultural subsidies and restrictions on your exports of agricultural products if we can have free access to your markets for industrial goods and services'. The bargain goes by the name of NAMA (non-agricultural market access), and was first launched at the Doha meeting of the WTO in 2001, which was supposed to be an Agenda for Development but, as Pascal Lamy, Director General of the WTO, said in 2007, has turned out to be about trade-offs not about morals. It is designed to reduce and eliminate all tariffs on industrial goods so that rich countries can penetrate poor country markets, and in return rich countries promise to reduce protection of their agricultural sectors. Close inspection of the deal, however, reveals that greater access by poor countries to rich countries' agricultural markets is not worth the tariff reductions that rich countries want to exploit the manufacturing and service sectors of developing countries. Firstly, many poor developing countries are overall net-importers of food so that a reduction in agricultural subsidies will harm them. The only developing countries that are likely to benefit from lower agricultural tariffs are big food exporters, such as Brazil and Argentina, which are large exporters of wheat, beef and dairy products. Rich countries do not mind reducing tariffs on many commodities such as coffee, tea, cocoa, and so on because they do not produce these goods themselves. Indeed, importing them duty-free raises the effective rate of protection on their processing. Secondly, many poor developing countries already benefit from trade preferences, Thirdly, poor countries agreeing to reduce tariffs on all industrial imports is denying the chance of these countries ever industrialising; to produce a range of manufactured goods that will promote overall development. In fact 11 countries (Argentina, Venezuela, Egypt, India, Indonesia, Namibia, Philippines, South Africa and Tunisia) have now formed an alliance (NAMA-11) to resist big tariff reductions demanded by the developed countries on the grounds that they need to protect industrial development and employment in their countries. They are rightly worried that such cuts will lead to deindustrialisation and job losses, particularly in sectors such as automobiles, textiles, clothing, footwear, leather, plastics, rubber and metals. The trade unions in these countries have also formed an alliance to ensure that their governments stand firm and do not sacrifice the possibility of industrial development for small gains in agriculture.

Poor developing countries need their 'policy space' to promote non-traditional outputs and exports in their own way. The Doha round of trade talks, that have been ongoing since 2001, ultimately collapsed on 29 July 2008 under this Faustian bargain. What is needed are not new deals which weaken the ability of poor countries to protect themselves even further from the onslaught of rich countries, but a new world trade order which acts on behalf of poor countries and recognises their needs. This also means that the poor developing countries need a much louder voice and participation in setting the agenda for trade reform. For too long, the agenda has been set largely by developed countries to promote their own interests (for example the switch of emphasis for the Doha round from goods to high-skill services, capital flows and international property rights). Not only has the agenda been unfair, but also the trade negotiations themselves and their enforcement of rules have not been fair. Poor developing countries do not have the resources and expertise to negotiate on equal terms and are often put under intense pressure by the rich countries. Poor countries cannot easily enforce decisions made in their favour when rules have been broken. A development agenda, drawn up by the developing countries themselves, would focus on the free access to the markets of developed countries; the end of agricultural subsidies in developed countries; allowing unskilled labour to migrate to richer countries; and allowing more trade in labour-intensive services such as construction and transport. Today's international trading system was not pre-ordained; it has been man-made, reflecting political choices, but for a multitude of reasons the voice of poor countries has not been heard or heeded. But the world has choices. It can continue to give preference to the interests of countries already rich and powerful, or it can attempt to address the gross inequalities in the world economy by giving priority to the needs and interests of the poor and vulnerable.

Poor countries had much more 'policy space' under the General Agreement on Tariffs and Trade (GATT) that preceded the establishment of the World Trade Organization (WTO) in 1995 (Wade,

2003). If trade is to promote development, the WTO needs radical reform and rethinking. The Agreement establishing the WTO lists as one of its purposes:

> raising standards of living, ensuring full employment and a large and steady growing volume of real income and effective demand, and expanding the production of, and trade in, goods and services, while allowing for the optimal use of the world's resources in accordance with the objective of sustainable development, seeking both to protect and preserve the environment and to enhance the means of doing so in a manner consistent with their respective needs and concerns at different levels of economic development. (WTO, 1995, p. 9)

The aim is laudable, but unfortunately there is a divorce between reality and rhetoric because the WTO treats as synonymous trade liberalisation and economic development; and yet as we have seen the historical and contemporary evidence is that domestic economic policy, institution-building and the promotion of investment opportunities are far more important than trade liberalisation and trade openness in determining economic success in the early stages of economic development. Rodrik (2001) reminds us (like Chang, 2002, 2005 and Reinert, 2007) that 'no country has [ever] developed simply by opening itself up to foreign trade and investment. The trick has been to combine the opportunities offered by world markets with a domestic investment and institution-building strategy to stimulate the animal spirits of domestic entrepreneurs'. But, now, under WTO rules, all the things that, for example, Korea, Taiwan and other East Asian countries did to promote economic growth in the 1960s, 1970s and 1980s are severely restricted; for example, the protection of domestic markets, export subsidies, domestic content requirements for FDI, tax rebates on imported inputs, and so on. Some countries that 'break' the rules are succeeding spectacularly. China is one obvious example, but another would be Vietnam which, while promoting FDI and exports, also protects its domestic market, maintains import monopolies and engages in State trading. Rodrik (2001) sets out five simple principles that should govern a world trading system designed to promote development as an alternative to the principles of the WTO:

1. Trade should be seen as a means to an end, not an end in itself. Instead of asking what kind of multilateral trading system maximises foreign trade and investment, the question that should be asked is what kind of multilateral system best serves the needs of poor countries.
2. Trade rules should allow for diversity in national institutions and standards. Poor countries need policy space for their own development strategies, and rich countries should not impose their institutional preferences on others.
3. Non-democratic countries should not count on the same trade privileges as democratic countries, particularly where the exports of these

countries hurt importing countries and are being produced under conditions which do not meet minimum labour standards, safety standards, and so on.

4. Countries have the right to protect their own institutions and development priorities. For example, poor countries should be allowed to subsidise industrial activities (and exports) if this is part of a development strategy to stimulate technological capacity, or be allowed to impose (temporary) protection if a vital industry is threatened by imports. The WTO has a 'safeguard' system in place to protect industries from import surges, but its use is very circumscribed. Rodrik suggests an *Agreement on Developmental and Social Safeguards* which would allow a country to exercise an 'opt-out' from WTO rules if it was agreed by all parties concerned – importers, exporters and consumers – that such action was in the broad economic and social interest of the country.

5. Countries should not have the right to impose their own institutional preferences on others. Trade sanctions or threats are not the way to alter countries' institutional behaviour. This is much better done through diplomacy or foreign policy.

In short 'the [WTO] trade regime must accept, rather than seek to eliminate, institutional diversity, along with the rights of countries to "protect" their institutional arrangements'. The WTO should shift away from trying to maximise the flow of trade to understanding and evaluating what trade regime will maximise the possibility of development for poor countries.

It is not only in trade in physical goods that there is a divorce between rhetoric and reality, but also in areas such as intellectual property rights, foreign direct investment, and trade in services, where many of the rules of the WTO protect the interest of rich countries and multinational corporations to the detriment of the poor. Prime examples are TRIPS (Trade-Related Aspects of Intellectual Property Rights), TRIMS (Trade-Related Investment Measures) and GATS (General Agreement on Trade in Services). TRIPS give more stringent protection for patents taken out in developed countries which raises the cost of technology transfers to poor countries in a variety of different fields. It raises the cost of medicines to fight disease and poverty. It raises the cost of new technologies to farmers, including seeds, fertilisers and pesticides, which otherwise could raise agricultural productivity. Multinational companies even have the right to patent genetic materials taken from the poor countries themselves. No wonder Oxfam (2002) has described the TRIPS agreement as 'an act of institutional fraud'. GATS is designed to allow rich countries to penetrate the service sector of poor countries, including banking and financial services, and the provision of basic utilities such as water and electricity. The privatisation of such service by foreign investors can severely hurt the poor. Poor people have the right to the provision of basic needs at affordable prices, and the supply of these public goods needs to be retained in domestic hands. Neither TRIPS, TRIMs nor GATS are designed to serve the needs of the poor, but rather vested interests in rich countries. As Rodrik (2001) says:

> WTO rules on anti-dumping, subsidies and countervailing measures, agriculture, textiles, trade-related investment measures (TRIMS) and trade-related property rights (TRIPS) are utterly devoid of any economic rational beyond the mercantilist interests of a narrow set of powerful groups in the advanced industrial countries. The *development* (emphasis added) pay-off of most of these requirements is hard to see.[3] (p. 27)

To grow out of poverty, poor countries need easy access to technology that will improve health, raise productivity in agriculture, and lead to the creation of new industries. UNCTADS's *Least Developed Countries Report 2007* on the topic of 'Knowledge, Technological Learning and Innovation for Development' (UNCTAD, 2007) remarks that

> most least developed countries (LDCs) [fifty of them] have opened their economies and are now highly integrated with the rest of the world . . . but even where they are increasing exports and attracting foreign investments, most LDCs are not climbing the economic and technological ladder. Their economies remain locked into low value-added commodity production and low-skill manufacturing.[4] (p. 7)

What to do? We need to remember both the economic history of the now-developed countries and straightforward economic theory, and not be shy of rehearsing the economic arguments for protection, particularly the infant industry argument and cases where the social cost of labour is less than the private cost, or where social benefits exceed private benefits in the case of knowledge spillovers from investment in research and development and increased investment in conditions of uncertainty (the Hausmann–Rodrik argument). Countries need time to build new productive capacity. Chang (2007) reminds us that it took South Korea and Japan 20–30 years to develop its world class industries. Countries also need to be free to make mistakes. Even if enterprises never achieve low enough costs to adequately compete in international markets, it may be better to have some inefficient industries with high levels of employment than no industries at all. Even inefficient industries can have spillover effects for the rest of the economy which most traditional (agriculture-based) activities do not. Countries should be free to choose which activities to protect and promote, and not be dictated to by countries that did not practice what they preach. Countries need policy space, one aspect of which is the promotion of 'self-discovery'. In the last resort, only structural changes will make poor countries rich.

We will leave the final word to Nobel Laureate, Joseph Stiglitz (2006):

> Trade liberalisation has not lived up to its promise. But the basic logic of trade – its potential to make most, if not all,

better off – remains. Trade is not a zero-sum game in which those who win do so at the cost of others; it is, or at least can be, a positive-sum game, in which everyone can be a winner. If that potential is to be realised, first we must reject two of the long-standing premises of trade liberalisation: that trade liberalisation automatically leads to more trade and growth, and that growth will automatically 'trickle down' to benefit all. Neither is consistent with economic theory or historical experience. (pp. 99–100)

Notes

1. Except for Chile, which liberalised slowly, and Venezuela buoyed up by oil.
2. See also, UNDP (2003).
3. For a full discussion of intellectual property rights see Chapter 3 of the 2007 LDCs Report (UNCTAD, 2007) written by Zeljka Kozul-Wright.
4. Quoted from the Executive Summary Press Release.

Bibliography

Abramovitz, M. (1986), Catching Up, Forging Ahead, and Falling Behind, *Journal of Economic History*, June.

Agosin, M.R. (1991), Trade Policy Reform and Economic Performance: A Review of the Issues and Some Preliminary Evidence, *UNCTAD Discussion Papers*, No. 41 (Geneva: UNCTAD).

Ahmed, N.U. (2000), Export Responses to Trade Liberalisation in Bangladesh: A Cointegration Analysis, *Applied Economics*, June.

Amin, S. (1974), *Accumulation on a World Scale: A Critique of the Theory of Underdevelopment* (New York: Monthly Review Press).

Amsden, A. (2001), *The Rise of the 'Rest': Challenges to the West from Late-Industrialising Economies* (Oxford: Oxford University Press).

Anderson, E. (2005), Openness and Inequality in Developing Countries: A Review of Theory and Recent Evidence, *World Development*, July.

Arbache, J., Dickerson, A. and Green, F. (2004), Trade Liberalisation and Wages in Developing Countries, *Economic Journal*, February.

Bairoch, P. (1972), Free Trade and European Economic Development in the 19th Century, *European Economic Review*, November.

Bairoch, P. (1975), *The Economic Development of the Third World Since 1900* (London: Methuen).

Bairoch, P. (1993), *Economics and World History – Myths and Paradoxes* (Brighton: Harvester Wheatsheaf).

Balassa, B. (1971), *The Structure of Protection in Developing Countries* (Baltimore MD: John Hopkins University Press).

Baldwin, R. (ed.) (1988), *Trade Policy Issues and Empirical Analysis* (Chicago: Chicago University Press for the NBER).

Barro, R. (1991), Economic Growth in a Cross Section of Countries, *Quarterly Journal of Economics*, May.

Barro, R. (2000), Inequality and Growth in a Panel of Countries, *Journal of Economic Growth*, March.

Ben David, D. (1993), Equalising Exchange: Trade Liberalisation and Income Convergence, *Quarterly Journal of Economics*, August.

Ben David, D. (1996), Trade and Convergence Among Countries, *Journal of International Economics*, May.

Bernard, A. and Jones, C. (1996), Comparing Apples to Oranges: Productivity Convergence and Measurement Across Industries and Countries, *American Economic Review*, September.

Bertola, G. and Faini, R. (1991), Import Demand and Non-Tariff Barriers: The Impact of Trade Liberalisation, *Journal of Development Economics*, November.

Besley, T. and Burgess, R. (2003), Halving Global Poverty, *Journal of Economic Perspectives*, Summer.

Bhagwati, J. (1958), Immiserising Growth: A Geometric Note, *Review of Economic Studies*, June.

Bhagwati, J. (1978), *Anatomy and Consequences of Exchange Control Regimes Vol. 1*, Studies in International Economic Relations No. 10 (New York: NBER).

Bhagwati, J. (1988), *Protectionism* (Cambridge MA: MIT Press).

Bhagwati, J. (2001), *Free Trade Today* (New Jersey: Princeton University Press).

Bhagwati, J. and Ramaswami, V.K. (1963), Domestic Distortions, Tariffs and the Theory of the Optimum Subsidy, *Journal of Political Economy*, February.

Bhalla, S. (2002), *Imagine There is No Country*, (Washington DC: Institute for International Economics).

Bleaney, M. (1999), Trade Reform, Macroeconomic Performance and Export Growth in Ten Latin American Countries 1979–95, *Journal of International Trade and Economic Development*, March.

Bosworth, B. and Collins, S. (2004), The Empirics of Growth: An Update, *Brookings Papers on Economic Activity*, No. 2.

Bourguignon, F. and Morrisson, C. (2002), Inequality Among World Citizens: 1820–1992, *American Economic Review*, September.

Buffie, E. (2001), *Trade Policy in Developing Countries* (Cambridge: Cambridge University Press).

Campo, J.A. and Taylor, L. (1998), Trade Liberalisation in Developing Economies: Modest Benefits but Problems with Productivity Growth, Macro Prices, and Income Distribution, *Economic Journal*, September.

Cashin, P. and McDermott, C.J. (2002), The Long Run Behaviour of Commodity Prices: Small Trends and Big Variability, *IMF Staff Papers*, May.

Chang, Ha-Joon (2002), *Kicking Away the Ladder: Development Strategy in Historical Perspective* (London: Anthem Press).

Chang, Ha-Joon (2005), *Why Developing Countries Need Tariffs?* (Geneva: South Centre).

Chang, Ha-Joon (2007), *Bad Samaritans: Rich Nations, Poor Policies and the Threat to the Developing World* (Random House Business Books).

Chen, S. and Ravallion, M. (2004), How Have the World's Poorest Fared Since the Early 1980s?, *The World Bank Research Observer*, Fall.

Christian Aid (2005), The Economics of Failure: The Real Cost of Free Trade for Poor Countries, Briefing Paper, June.

Clarke, R. and Kirkpatrick, C. (1992), 'Trade Policy Reform and Economic Performance in Developing Countries: Assessing the Empirical Evidence', in R. Adhikari, C. Kirkpatrick and J. Weiss (eds), *Industrial and Trade Policy Reform in Developing Countries* (Manchester: Manchester University Press).

Clemens, M. and Williamson, J. (2001), A Tariff-Growth Paradox? – Protection's Impact the World Around 1875–1997, NBER Working Paper No. 8459, (Cambridge MA: National Bureau of Economic Research).

Cline, W. (1997), *Trade and Income Distribution* (Washington: Institute for International Economics).

Corden, M. (1966), The Structure of a Tariff System and the Effective Protection Rate, *Journal of Political Economy*, May/June.

Corden, M. (1971), *The Theory of Protection* (Oxford: Clarendon Press).

Cornia, A. and Kiiski, S. (2001), Trends in Income Distribution in the Post World War II Period, *WIDER Discussion Paper*, 89 (Helsinki: WIDER).

Dean, J., Desai, S. and Reidel, J. (1994), Trade Policy Reform in Developing Countries Since 1985: A Review of the Evidence, World Bank Development Policy Group, mimeo.

Deininger, L. and Squire, L. (1996), A New Data Set Measuring Income Inequality, *World Bank Economic Review*, September.

Dixon, R.J. and Thirlwall, A.P. (1975), A Model of Regional Growth Rate Differences on Kaldorian Lines, *Oxford Economic Papers*, July.

Dollar, D. (1992), Outward Oriented Developing Countries Really do Grow More Rapidly: Evidence from 95 LDCs 1976–85, *Economic Development and Cultural Change*, April.

Dollar, D. (2005), Globalisation, Poverty and Inequalities since 1980, *The World Bank Research Observer*, Fall.

Dollar, D. and Kraay, A. (2002), Growth *Is* Good for the Poor, *Journal of Economic Growth*, September.

Dollar, D. and Kraay, A. (2004), Trade, Growth and Poverty, *Economic Journal*, February.

Dornbusch, R. (1992), The Case for Trade Liberalisation in Developing Countries, *Journal of Economic Perspectives*, Winter.

Dos Santos, T. (1970), The Structure of Dependence, *American Economic Review, Papers and Proceedings*, May.

Dowrick, S. (1997), 'Trade and Growth: A Survey', in J. Fagerberg, P. Hansson, L. Lundberg and A. Melchior (eds), *Trade, Technology, and Changes in Employment of Skilled Labour in Swedish Manufacturing* (Cheltenham, UK and Lyme, USA: Edward Elgar).

Dowrick, S. and Golley, J. (2004), Trade Openness and Growth: Who Benefits?, *Oxford Review of Economic Policy*, Spring.

Edward, P. (2006), Examining Inequality: Who Really Benefits from Global Growth?, *World Development*, October.

Edwards, S. (1992), Trade Orientation, Distortions and Growth in Developing Countries, *Journal of Development Economics*, July.

Edwards, S. (1993), Openness, Trade Liberalisation and Growth in Developing Countries, *Journal of Economic Literature*, September.

Edwards, S. (1998), Openness, Productivity and Growth: What Do We Really Know? *Economic Journal*, March.

Emmanuel, A. (1972), *Unequal Exchange: A Study of the Imperialism of Trade* (New York: Monthly Review Press).

Esfahani, H. (1991), Exports, Imports, and Economic Growth in Semi-Industrialised Countries, *Journal of Development Economics*, January.

Feder, G. (1983), On Exports and Economic Growth, *Journal of Development Economics*, February/April.

Feenstra, R. and Hanson, G. (1996), 'Foreign Investment, Outsourcing and Relative Wages', in R. Feenstra, G. Grossman and D. Irwin (eds), *Political Economy of Trade Policy: Essays in Honour of Jagdish Bhagwati* (Cambridge MA: MIT Press).

Feenstra, R. and Hanson, G. (1997), Foreign Direct Investment and Relative Wages: Evidence from Mexico's Maquiladoras, *Journal of International Economics*, May.

Fielden, K. (1969), 'The Rise and Fall of Free Trade', in C. Bartlett (ed.), *Britain Pre-eminent: Studies in British World Influence in the Nineteenth Century* (London: Macmillan).

Fischer, S. (2003), Globalisation and Its Challenges, *American Economic Review*, May.

Frank, G. (1967), *Capitalism and Underdevelopment in Latin America* (New York: Monthly Review Press).

Freeman, R. and Oostendrop, R. (2001), The Occupational Wages Around the World Data File, *International Labour Review*, Vol. 140, No. 4.

Friedman, M. (1990) (with R. Friedman), *Free to Choose* (New York: Harcourt Brace).

Galbraith, J. and Liu, L. (2001), 'Measuring the Evolution of Inequalities in the Global Economy', in J. Galbraith and M. Berner (eds), *Inequality and Industrial Change: A Global View* (New York: Cambridge University Press).

Ghose, A. (2004), Global Inequality and International Trade, *Cambridge Journal of Economics*, March.

Goldberg, P. and Pavcnik, N. (2004), Trade, Inequality and Poverty: What do we Know? Evidence from Recent Trade Liberalisation Episodes in Developing Countries, NBER Working Paper No. 10593.

Goldberg, P. and Pavcnik, N. (2007), Distributional Effects of Globalisation in Developing Countries, *Journal of Economic Literature*, March.

Goulet, D. (1971), *The Cruel Choice: A New Concept in the Theory of Development* (New York: Atheneum).

Goulet, D. (1995), *Development Ethics: A Guide to Theory and Practice* (London: Zed Books Ltd).

Green, F., Dickerson, A. and Arbache, J. (2001), A Picture of Wage Inequality and the Allocation of Labour Through a Period of Trade Liberalisation:

The Case of Brazil, *World Development*, November.

Greenaway, D. (1993), Liberalising Foreign Trade through Rose Tinted Glasses, *Economic Journal*, January.

Greenaway, D. and Nam, C.H. (1988), Industrialisation and Macroeconomic Performance in Developing Countries under Alternative Trade Strategies, *Kyklos*, August.

Greenaway, D. and Sapsford, D. (1994), What Does Liberalisation do for Exports and Growth, *Weltwirtschaftliches Archiv (Review of World Economics)*, March.

Greenaway, D., Leybourne, S. and Sapsford, D. (1997), Modelling Growth (and Liberalisation) Using Smooth Transition Analysis, *Economic Inquiry*, October.

Greenaway, D., Morgan, W. and Wright, P. (1997), Trade Liberalisation and Growth in Developing Countries: Some New Evidence, *World Development*, November.

Greenaway, D., Morgan, W. and Wright, P. (1998), Trade Reform, Adjustment and Growth: What Does the Evidence Tell Us?, *Economic Journal*, September.

Greenaway, D., Morgan, W. and Wright, P. (2002), Trade Liberalisation and Growth in Developing Countries, *Journal of Development Economics*, February.

Grossman, G. and Helpman, E. (1991a), *Innovation and Growth in the Global Economy* (Cambridge MA: MIT Press).

Grossman, G. and Helpman, E. (1991b), Trade, Knowledge Spillovers and Growth, *European Economic Review*, April.

Gylfason, J. (2001), Nature, Power and Growth, *Scottish Journal of Political Economy*, November.

Hagen, E. (1988), An Economic Justification of Protectionism, *Quarterly Journal of Economics*, November.

Hamilton, A. (1791), *Report on the Subject of Manufactures*, 5 December 1791. Reprinted in *Alexander Hamilton – Writings* (New York: The Library Classics of the United States, Inc. 2001).

Hanson, G. and Harrison, A. (1999), Trade Liberalisation and Wage Inequality in Mexico, *Industrial and Labour Relations Review*, January.

Harberger, A. (1954), Monopoly and Resource Allocation, *American Economic Review, Papers and Proceedings*, May.

Harrison, A. (1996), Openness and Growth: A Time Series, Cross-Country Analysis for Developing Countries, *Journal of Development Economics*, March.

Harrison, A. and Hanson, G. (1999), Who Gains from Trade Reform? Some Remaining Puzzles, *Journal of Development Economics*, June.

Harrod, R. (1933), *International Economics* (London: Macmillan).

Hausmann, R. and Rodrik, D. (2003), Economic Development as Self Discovery, *Journal of Development Economics*, December.

Hausmann, R., Pritchett, L., and Rodrik, D. (2005), Growth Accelerations, *Journal of Economic Growth*, December.

Hayek, F. Von (1949), *Individualism and Economic Order* (Chicago: University of Chicago Press).

Heckscher, E. (1919), The Effect of Foreign Trade on the Distribution of Income, *Ekonomisk Tidskrift*, Vol. 21.

Helleiner, G.K. (ed.) (1994), *Trade Policy and Industrialization in Turbulent Times* (London: Routledge).

Helpman, E. and Krugman, P. (1985), *Market Structure and Foreign Trade* (Cambridge MA: MIT Press).

Helpman, E. and Krugman, P. (1989), *Trade Policy and Market Structure* (Cambridge MA: MIT Press).

Hicks, J. (1959), *Essays in World Economics* (Oxford: Clarendon Press).

Higgins, M. and Williamson, J. (1999), Explaining Inequality the World Round: Cohort Size, Kuznets Curves and Openness, NBER Working Paper No. 7224 (Cambridge MA).

Hirschman, A. (1958), *Strategy of Economic Development* (New Haven: Yale University Press).

IMF (1998), Trade Liberalisation in IMF Supported Programmes, *World Economic and Financial Surveys* (Washington DC: IMF).

Jenkins, R. (1996), Trade Liberalisation and Export Performance in Bolivia, *Development and Change*, April.

Johnson, H. (1964), Tariffs and Economic Development: Some Theoretical Issues, *Journal of Development Studies*, October.

Johnson, H. (1965), 'Optimal Trade Intervention in the Presence of Domestic Distortions', in R. Baldwin et al. (eds), *Trade, Growth and the Balance of Payments: Essays in Honour of Gottfried Haberler* (Chicago: Rand McNally).

Jones, C. (1997), On the Evolution of the World Income Distribution, *Journal of Economic Perspectives*, Summer.

Joshi, V. and Little, I.M.D. (1996), *India's Economic Reforms 1991–2001* (Oxford: Oxford University Press).

Jung, W. and Marshall, P. (1985), Exports, Growth and Causality in Developing Countries, *Journal of Development Economics*, May–June.

Kaldor, N. (1970), The Case for Regional Policies, *Scottish Journal of Political Economy*, November.

Keynes, J.M. (1933), National Self Sufficiency, *New Statesman and Nation*, 8 and 13 July.

Keynes, J.M. (1936), *The General Theory of Employment, Interest and Money* (London: Macmillan).

Khan, M. and Knight, M. (1983), Determinants of Current Account Balances of Non-Oil Developing Countries in the 1970s, *IMF Staff Papers*, December.

Khan, M. and Zahler, R. (1985), Trade and Financial Liberalisation Given External Shocks and Inconsistent Domestic Policies, *IMF Staff Papers*, March.

Kneller, R. (2007), No Miracles Here: Trade Policy, Fiscal Policy and Economic Growth, *Journal of Development Studies*, October.

Knight, M., Loayza, N. and Villanueva, D. (1993), Testing the Neoclassical Theory of Economic Growth, *IMF Staff Papers*, September.

Krueger, A. (1978), *Foreign Trade Regimes and Economic Development: Liberalisation Attempts and Consequences* (Lexington MA: Baltinger Press for NBER).

Krueger, A. (1997), Trade Policy and Economic Development: How We Learn, *American Economic Review*, March.

Krueger, A. (1998), Why Trade Liberalisation is Good for Growth, *Economic Journal*, September.

Krugman, P. (1984), 'Import Protection as Export Promotion: International Competition in the Presence of Oligopoly and Economies of Scale', in H. Kierzkowski (ed.), *Monopolistic Competition in International Trade* (Oxford: Clarendon Press).

Krugman, P. (1986), *Strategic Trade Policy and the New International Economics* (Cambridge MA: MIT Press).

Krugman, P. (1987), Is Free Trade Passé?, *Journal of Economic Perspectives*, Fall.

Krugman, P. (1989), Differences in Income Elasticities and Trends in Real Exchange Rates, *European Economic Review*, May.

Krugman, P. (1991), *Geography and Trade* (Cambridge MA: MIT Press).

Krugman, P. (1993a), The Narrow and Broad Arguments for Free Trade, *American Economic Review, Papers and Proceedings*, May.

Krugman, P. (1993b), What do Undergrads Need to Know about Trade? *American Economic Review, Papers and Proceedings*, May.

Krugman, P. (1994), *Rethinking International Trade* (Cambridge MA: MIT Press).

Krugman, P. (1995), *Development, Geography and Economic Theory* (Cambridge MA: MIT Press).

Krugman, P. and Smith, A. (1994), *Empirical Studies of Strategic Trade Policy* (Chicago: University of Chicago Press).

Krugman, P. and Venables, A. (1995), Globalization and the Inequality of Nations, *Quarterly Journal of Economics*, November.

Kuznets, S. (1955), Economic Growth and Income Inequality, *American Economic Review*, March.

Leamer, E. (1988), 'Measures of Openness', in R. Baldwin (ed.), *Trade Policy Issues and Empirical Analysis* (Chicago: Chicago University Press).

Leontief, W. (1953), Domestic Production and Foreign Trade: The American Position Re-examined, *Proceedings of the American Philosophical Society*, September.

Lerner, J. and Van der Berg, H. (2003), How Large is International Trade's Effect on Economic Growth?, *Journal of Economic Surveys*, July.

Levine, R. and Renelt, D. (1992), A Sensitivity Analysis of Cross-Country Growth Regressions, *American Economic Review*, September.

Lewis, A. (1954), Economic Development with Unlimited Supplies of Labour, *Manchester School*, May.

Li, H., Squire, L. and Zou, H. (1998), Explaining International and Intertemporal Variations in Income Inequality, *Economic Journal*, January.

List, F. (1841), *The National System of Political Economy* (translated by S.S. Lloyd) (Fairfield, NJ: Augustus M. Kelley 1991).

List, F. (1885), *The National System of Political Economy*, translated from the original German edition published in 1841 by Sampson Lloyd (London: Longmann, Green and Company).

Little, I.M.D. and Mirrlees, J. (1974), *Project Appraisal and Planning for Developing Countries* (London: Heinemann).

Little, I.M.D., Scitovsky, T. and Scott, M. (1970), *Industry and Trade in Some Developing Countries* (London and New York: Oxford University Press for OECD).

Loser, C. and Guerguil, M. (1999), Trade and Trade Reform in Latin America and the Caribbean in the 1990s, *Journal of Applied Economics*, May.

Maddison, A. (1995), *Monitoring the World Economy 1820–1992* (Paris: OECD).

Maddison, A. (2001), *The World Economy, A Millennial Perspective* (Paris: OECD).

Maddison, A. (2003), *The World Economy: Historical Statistics* (Paris: Development Centre Studies, OECD).

Mah, J.S. (1999), Import Demand, Liberalisation and Economic Development, *Journal of Policy Modelling*, July.

Malhortan, K. et al. (2003), *Making Global Trade Work for People* (London: Earthscan).

Marshall, A. (1890), *Principles of Economics* (London: Macmillan).

Mbabazi, J., Morrissey, O. and Milner, C. (2003), 'The Fragility of Empirical Links Between Inequality, Trade Liberalisation, Growth and Poverty', in R. van der Hoeven and A. Shorrocks (eds), *Perspectives on Growth and Poverty* (Tokyo: United Nations University Press).

McCombie, J.S.L. and Thirlwall, A.P. (1994), *Economic Growth and the Balance of Payments Constraint* (London: Macmillan).

McCombie, J.S.L. and Thirlwall, A.P. (1997), The Dynamic Harrod Trade Multiplier and the Demand Oriented Approach to Economic Growth: An Evaluation, *International Review of Applied Economics*, January.

McCombie, J.S.L. and Thirlwall, A.P. (2004), *Essays on Balance of Payments Constrained Growth: Theory and Evidence* (London: Routledge).

Melo, O. and Vogt, M.G. (1984), Determinants of the Demand for Imports of Venezuela, *Journal of Development Economics*, April.

Michaely, M., Papageorgiou, D. and Choksi, A. (eds) (1991), *Liberalising Foreign Trade, Vol. 7: Lessons of Experience in the Developing World* (Oxford: Basil Blackwell).

Milanovic, B. (2005a), Can we Discern the Effect of Globalisation on Income Distribution? *The World Bank Economic Review*, January.

Milanovic, B. (2005b), *Worlds Apart: Measuring International and Global Inequality* (Princeton NJ: Princeton University Press).

Mill, J.S. (1848), *Principles of Political Economy* (London: Longmans, Green and Co.).

Moggridge, D. (1981), *The Collected Writings of J.M. Keynes Vol. 20: Activities 1929–1931: Rethinking Employment and Unemployment Policies* (London: Macmillan).

Myrdal, G. (1957), *Economic Theory and Underdeveloped Regions* (London: Duckworth).

O'Rourke, K. (2000), Tariffs and Growth in the Late 19th Century, *Economic Journal*, April.

O'Rourke, K. (2001), Globalisation and Inequality: Historical Trends, NBER Working Paper No. 8339.

Ocampo, J. and Taylor, L. (1998), Trade Liberalisation in Developing Economies: Modest Benefits but Problems with Productivity Growth, Macro Prices, and Income Distribution, *Economic Journal*, September.

Ohlin, B. (1933), *Interregional and International Trade* (Cambridge MA: Harvard University Press).

Ostry, J. and Rose, D. (1992), An Empirical Evaluation of the Macroeconomic Effects of Tariffs, *Journal of International Money and Finance*, February.

Oxfam (2002), *Rigged Rules and Double Standards: Trade, Globalisation and the Fight Against Poverty* (Oxford: Oxfam).

Pacheco-López, P. (2005), The Impact of Trade Liberalisation on Exports, Imports, the Balance of Payments and Growth: The Case of Mexico, *Journal of Post Keynesian Economics*, Summer.

Pacheco-López, P. and Thirlwall, A.P. (2004), Trade Liberalisation in Mexico: Rhetoric and Reality, *Banca Nazionale del Lavoro Quarterly Review*, June.

Pacheco-López, P. and Thirlwall, A.P. (2006), Trade Liberalisation, the Income Elasticity of Demand for Imports and Growth in Latin America, *Journal of Post Keynesian Economics*, Fall.

Pacheco-López, P. and Thirlwall, A.P. (2007), Trade Liberalisation and the Trade-Off Between Growth and the Balance of Payments in Latin America, *International Review of Applied Economics*, September.

Pack, H. (1988), 'Industrialisation and Trade', in H. Chenery and T.N. Srinivasan (eds), *Handbook of Development Economics, Vol. 1* (Amsterdam: North Holland).

Papageorgiou, D., Michaely, M. and Choksi, A. (eds) (1991), *Liberalising Foreign Trade* (Oxford: Basil Blackwell).

Parikh, A. (2002), Impact of Liberalization, Economic Growth and Trade Policies on Current Accounts of Developing Countries: An Econometric Study, WDP 2002/63 (Helsinki: WIDER).

Parikh, A. and Shibata, M. (2007), 'Does Trade Liberalisation Accelerate Convergence in Per

Capita Incomes in Developing Countries?', in A. Parikh (ed.), *Trade Liberalisation: Impact on Growth and Trade in Developing Countries* (London: World Scientific).

Prebisch, R. (1950), *The Economic Development of Latin America and its Principal Problems* (New York: ECLA, UN Dept of Economic Affairs).

Prebisch, R. (1959), Commercial Policy in the Underdeveloped Countries, *American Economic Review, Papers and Proceedings*, May.

Pritchett, L. (1996), Measuring Outward Orientation in LDCs: Can it be Done?, *Journal of Development Economics*, May.

Pritchett, L. (1997), Divergence: Big Time, *Journal of Economic Perspectives*, Summer.

Rajapatirana, S. (1998), 'Trade Policies, Macroeconomic Adjustment and Manufacturing Exports', in M.J. Lord (ed.), *The Handbook of Latin American Trade in Manufacturing* (Cheltenham, UK and Lyme, USA: Edward Elgar).

Ravallion, M. (2001), Growth, Inequality and Poverty: Looking Beyond Averages, *World Development*, November.

Ravallion, M. (2006), Looking Beyond Averages in the Trade and Poverty Debate, *World Development*, August.

Redding, S. (1999), Dynamic Comparative Advantage and the Welfare Effects of Trade, *Oxford Economic Papers*, January.

Reinert, E. (2007), *How Rich Countries Got Rich and Why Poor Countries Stay Poor* (London: Constable and Robinson).

Reisen, H. (1998), Sustainable and Excessive Current Account Deficits, *Empirica*, January.

Ricardo, D. (1817), *On the Principles of Political Economy and Taxation* (P. Sraffa, ed.) (Cambridge University Press, 1951).

Rittenberg, L. (1986), Export Growth Performance of Less-Developed Countries, *Journal of Development Economics*, November.

Robbins, D. (1996), Evidence on Trade and Wages in the Developing World, *OECD Development Centre Technical Paper 119*, December.

Robertson, R. (2000), Trade Liberalisation and Wage Inequality: Lessons from the Mexican Experience, *World Economy*, June.

Rodriguez, F. and Rodrik, D. (2000), 'Trade Policy and Economic Growth: A Skeptic's Guide to the Cross-National Evidence', in B. Bernanke and K. Rogoff (eds), *Macroeconomics Annual 2000* (Cambridge MA: MIT Press).

Rodrik, D. (1988), 'Imperfect Competition, Scale Economies and Trade Policy in Developing Countries', in R. Baldwin (1988), op. cit.

Rodrik, D. (1989), Credibility of Trade Reform: A Policy Maker's Guide, *World Economy*, March.

Rodrik, D. (1992), The Limits of Trade Policy Reform in Developing Countries, *Journal of Economic Perspectives*, Winter.

Rodrik, D. (1996), Understanding Economic Policy Reform, *Journal of Economic Literature*, March.

Rodrik, D. (2001), *The Global Governance of Trade: As If Development Really Mattered* (New York: UNDP).

Rodrik, D. (2004), *Rethinking Growth Strategies*, WIDER Annual Lecture 8 (Helsinki: United Nations World Institute for Development Economics Research).

Romer, P. (1990), Endogenous Technical Change, *Journal of Political Economy*, October.

Sachs, J. (1987), 'Trade and Exchange Rate Policies in Growth-Oriented Adjustment Programs', in V. Corbo, M. Goldstein and M. Khan (eds), *Growth-Oriented Adjustment Programs* (Washington DC: IMF and World Bank).

Sachs, J. and Warner, A. (1995), Economic Reform and the Process of Global Integration, *Brookings Papers on Economic Activity No. 1*.

Sachs, J. and Warner, A. (1997), Sources of Slow Growth in African Economies, *Journal of African Economies*, October.

Sachs, J. and Warner, A. (2001), The Curse of Natural Resources, *European Economic Review*, May.

Sai-wing Ho, P. (2005), Distortions in the Trade Policy for Development Debate: A Re-examination of Friedrich List, *Cambridge Journal of Economics*, September.

Sala-i-Martin, X. (2002a), The Disturbing 'Rise' of Global Income Inequality, NBER Working Paper No. 8904.

Sala-i-Martin, X. (2002b), The World of Income, NBER Working Paper No. 8933, May.

Samuelson, P. (1948), International Trade and the Equalisation of Factor Prices, *Economic Journal*, June.

Samuelson, P. (1949), International Factor Price

Equalisation Once Again, *Economic Journal*, June.

Samuelson, P. (1962), Economists and the History of Ideas, *American Economic Review*, March.

Samuelson, P. (1971), Ohlin was Right, *Swedish Journal of Economics*, December.

Santos-Paulino, A. (2002a), Trade Liberalisation and Export Performance in Selected Developing Countries, *Journal of Development Studies*, October.

Santos-Paulino, A. (2002b), The Effects of Trade Liberalisation on Imports in Selected Developing Countries, *World Development*, June.

Santos-Paulino, A. (2004), Trade Liberalisation and the Balance of Payments in Selected Countries, *The Manchester School*, January.

Santos-Paulino, A. (2005), Trade Liberalisation and Economic Performance: Theory and Evidence, *World Economy*, June.

Santos-Paulino, A. (2007), Aid and Trade Sustainability under Liberalisation in Least Developed Countries, *World Economy*, June.

Santos-Paulino, A. and Thirlwall, A.P. (2004), The Impact of Trade Liberalisation on Exports, Imports, and the Balance of Payments of Developing Countries, *Economic Journal*, February.

Sarkar, P. and Singer, H. (1991, 1993), Manufactured Exports of Developing Countries and their Terms of Trade Since 1965, *World Development*, April and October.

Sen, A.K. (1999), *Development as Freedom* (Oxford: Oxford University Press).

Senghaas, D. (1985), *The European Experience: An*

Historical Critique of Development Theory (Leamington Spa, UK: Berg Publishers).

Shafaeddin, S.M. (1994), The Impact of Trade Liberalisation on Exports and GDP in Least Developed Countries, *UNCTAD Discussion Papers*, No. 85 (Geneva: UNCTAD).

Skarstein, R. (2007), Free Trade: A Dead End for Underdeveloped Countries, *Review of Political Economy*, July.

Singer, H. (1950), The Distribution of Gains Between Investing and Borrowing Countries, *American Economic Review*, May.

Smith, A. (1776), *An Inquiry into the Nature and Causes of the Wealth of Nations* (London: George Routledge and Sons).

Solow, R. (1956), A Contribution to the Theory of Economic Growth, *Quarterly Journal of Economics*, February.

Spilimbergo, A., Londoño, J.L. and Székely, M. (1999), Income Distribution, Factor Endowments and Trade Openness, *Journal of Development Economics*, June.

Stiglitz, J. (2002), *Globalisation and its Discontents* (London: Penguin Publishers).

Stiglitz, J. (2006), *Making Globalization Work* (New York: W.W. Norton and Co.).

Stolper, W. and Samuelson, P. (1941), Protection and Real Wages, *Review of Economic Studies*, November.

Subramanian, A. (2005), The Globalisation Curve: An Interview with Jagdish Bhagwati, *Finance and Development*, September.

Sutcliffe, B. (2004), World Inequality and Globalisation, *Oxford Review of Economic Policy*, Spring.

Suwa-Eisenmann, A. and Verdier, T. (2007), Aid and Trade, *Oxford Review of Economic Policy*, Autumn.

Svedberg, P. (2004), World Income Distribution: Which Way?, *Journal of Development Studies*, June.

Thirlwall, A.P. (1979), The Balance of Payments Constraint as an Explanation of International Growth Rate Differences, *Banca Nazionale del Lavoro Quarterly Review*, March.

Thirlwall, A.P. (1983), Foreign Trade Elasticities in Centre–Periphery Models of Growth and Development, *Banca Nazionale del Lavoro Quarterly Review*, September.

Thirlwall, A.P. (ed.) (1987), *Keynes and Economic Development* (London: Macmillan).

Thirlwall, A.P. (2002), *The Nature of Economic Growth: An Alternative Framework for Understanding the Performance of Nations* (Cheltenham, UK and Northampton, MA, USA: Edward Elgar).

Thirlwall, A.P. (2003), *Trade, the Balance of Payments and Exchange Rate Policy in Developing Countries* (Cheltenham, UK and Northampton, MA, USA: Edward Elgar).

Thirlwall, A.P. (2006), *Growth and Development: with Special Reference to Developing Economies*, 8th Edition (London: Palgrave-Macmillan).

Thomas, V., Nash, J. and Edwards, S. (1991), *Best Practices in Trade Policy Reform* (Oxford: Oxford University Press for the World Bank).

Torrens, R. (1833), *Letters on Commercial Policy* (London: Longman).

Tullock, G. (1967), The Welfare Costs of Tariffs, Monopoly and Theft, *Western Economic Journal*, June.

Tybout, J. (1992), Researching the Trade/Productivity Link: New Directions, *The World Bank Economic Review*, May.

UNCTAD (1989), *Trade and Development Report* (Geneva: United Nations).

UNCTAD (1999), *Trade and Development Report* (Geneva: United Nations).

UNCTAD (2004), *Least Developed Countries Report 2004: Linking International Trade with Poverty Reduction* (Geneva: United Nations).

UNCTAD (2007), *The Least Developed Countries Report 2007: Knowledge, Technological Learning and Innovation for Development* (Geneva: United Nations).

UNDP (1997), *Human Development Report* (Oxford: Oxford University Press).

UNDP (2003), *Making Global Trade Work for Poor People* (New York: Earthscan).

Vamvakidis, A. (2002), How Robust is the Growth – Openness Connection: Historical Evidence, *Journal of Economic Growth*, March.

Van den Berg, H. and Schmidt, J. (1994), Foreign Trade and Economic Growth: Time Series Evidence from Latin America, *Journal of International Trade and Economic Development*, November.

Van de Hoeven, R. and Shorrocks, A. (eds),

Perspectives on Growth and Poverty (Tokyo: United Nations Press).

Vos, R., Taylor, L. and Paes de Barros, R. (eds) (2002), *Economic Liberalisation, Distribution and Poverty: Latin America in the 1990s* (Cheltenham, UK and Northampton, MA, USA: Edward Elgar).

Wacziarg, R. (2001), Measuring the Dynamic Gains from Trade, *The World Bank Economic Review*, Vol. 15, No. 2.

Wacziarg, R. and Welch, K. (2005), Trade Liberalisation and Growth: New Evidence, NBER Working Paper No. 10152 (Cambridge MA: NBER).

Wade, R. (2001), The Rising Inequality of World Income Distribution, *Finance and Development*, December.

Wade, R. (2003), What Strategies are Viable for Developing Countries Today? The World Trade Organisation and the Shrinking of 'Development Space', *Review of International Political Economy*, November.

Wade, R. (2004), Is Globalisation Reducing Poverty and Inequality? *World Development*, April.

Wade, R. (2008), 'Globalisation, Growth, Poverty, Resentment and Imperialism', in J. Ravenhill (ed.) *Global Political Economy*, (Oxford: Oxford University Press).

Weiss, J. (1992), Export Response to Trade Reforms: Recent Mexican Experience, *Development Policy Review*, No. 10.

Williamson, J. (1993), Democracy and the Washington Consensus, *World Development*, August.

Winters, A., McCullock, N. and McKay, A. (2004), Trade Liberalisation and Poverty: the Evidence so Far, *Journal of Economic Literature*, March.

Winters, L. (2004), Trade Liberalisation and Economic Performance: An Overview, *Economic Journal*, February.

Wolf, H. (1993), Trade Orientation: Measurement and Consequences, *Estudios de Economía*, Vol. 20.

Wolf, M. (2005), *Why Globalisation Works* (New Haven: Yale University Press).

Wood, A. (1994), *North–South Trade, Employment and Inequality: Changing Fortunes in a Skill-Driven World* (Oxford: Clarendon Press).

Wood, A. (1995), How Trade Hurt Unskilled Workers, *Journal of Economic Perspectives*, Summer.

Wood, A. (1997), Openness and Wage Inequality in Developing Countries: The Latin American Challenge to East Asian Conventional Wisdom, *The World Bank Economic Review*, January.

Wood, A. (2002), Globalisation and Wage Inequalities: A Synthesis of Three Theories, *Weltwirtschaftliches Archiv (Review of World Economics)*, March.

World Bank (1987), *World Development Report 1987* (Washington DC: Oxford University Press).

World Bank (1991), *World Development Report 1991 – The Development Challenge* (New York: Oxford University Press).

World Bank (2002), *Globalization, Growth and Poverty* (Washington DC: Oxford University Press).

World Bank (1997, 2007), *World Development Indicators* (Washington DC: World Bank).

World Trade Organization (WTO) (1995), Agreement Establishing the World Trade Organization (Geneva: WTO Information and Media Relations Divisions).

Yanikkaya, H. (2003), Trade Openness and Economic Growth: A Cross-Country Empirical Investigation, *Journal of Development Economics*, October.

Zhu, S.C. and Trefler, D. (2005), Trade and Inequality in Developing Countries: A General Equilibrium Analysis, *Journal of International Economics*, January.

Index